NAVAL WAR COLLEGE
Illustrated History and Guide

EDITORS:
John E. Jackson
Jondavid DuVall
Kimberly Rhoades

Second Edition, April 2010.

Printed in the United States of America by U.S. Government Printing Office.

ISBN: 978-1-884733-72-7

For sale by the Superintendent of Documents, U.S. Government Printing Office
Internet: bookstore.gpo.gov Phone: toll free (866) 512-1800; DC area (202)512-1800
Fax: (202) 512-2104 Mail: Shop IDCC, Washington, DC 20402-0001

ISBN: 978-1-884733-72-7

About the Editors

John E. Jackson is a senior professor in the College of Distance Education. He served for 27 years as a Navy Supply Corps officer, and has served in teaching and management assignments at the Naval War College for a combined total of over 18 years. He holds advanced degrees from Providence College and Salve Regina University, and he is a graduate of the Management Development Program at Harvard University.

Major Jondavid DuVall, United States Air Force, is a logistics readiness officer and a recent graduate of the Naval War College, Newport, Rhode Island. Major DuVall entered the Air Force in 1991 and was commissioned in 1995 as a distinguished graduate of the Air Force Reserve Officer Training Corps at the University of North Carolina at Charlotte. He has previously worked at the squadron, wing, regional, and major command levels.

Major Kimberly Rhoades, United States Air Force, is a Services officer and a recent graduate of the Naval War College, Newport, Rhode Island. Major Rhoades entered into the Air Force in 1995 and was commissioned through the Officer Training School in 1996. She has held positions at the squadron, headquarters, and major command levels in both garrison and deployed locations.

NOTE: Edition I was completed as a Directed Research Project during the 2007–2008 academic year. Edition II was revised and updated in conjunction with the Naval War College's 125th Anniversary celebration during academic year 2009–2010.

Acknowledgments for the First Edition

We would like to acknowledge the following people for their gracious time, help, and support to bring this work to fruition. First and foremost, we would like to thank our academic advisor, Dr. John B. Hattendorf; without his help, guidance, and previous extensive research, this work would not be possible in a trimester's time. Our Senior Air Force Advisor, Colonel Kevin Darnell, for sharing the same vision we had. Dr. Evelyn Cherpak, Naval War College archivist, for help with documents concerning Medal of Honor recipients, graduates, and significant events in the history of the College. Professor Theodore Gatchel for his inspiration to dig deeper and exhaust our researching methods to find all of the Navy graduates who earned the Medal of Honor. *Semper Fi!*

We would like to thank the President of the Naval War College, for allowing us the opportunity to explain our project and gain his valuable insight, knowledge and guidance. Professor John Jackson for his information and inspiration on the Patriots Memorial, the Distinguished Graduate Leadership Award and as a contributing editor. Major Eric Bovasso for his research support and contribution in finalizing our Alumni chapter and contemporary issues. Commander Karen D. Sellers and the Public Affairs staff who helped immensely with reviewing content for printing and release, providing school photos and several flag officer interviews used in the Reflections section. Ms. Carolyn Harney was gracious enough to assist in editing numerous revisions and her insight and skills allowed us to produce a work worthy of publication. Ms. Gigi Davis and Mr. Joe Quinn for graphics and photography support. Mr. Wayne Rowe and the library staff for assisting us in hours of research.

Our sincerest thanks to Admiral Gary Roughead, Chief of Naval Operations, for his continued support of the Naval War College and its students from all services.

Acknowledgments for the Second Edition

Building upon the superb work done by Majors DuVall and Rhoades, we have attempted to update the History and Guide to bring it current to the College's anniversary year. Thanks again to Dr. John Hattendorf, and to the skilled artisans in the Visual Communications and Desktop Publishing departments.

Contents

Introduction 1

I. History 2

II. Presidents 12

III. Missions and Traditions 30

IV. Heroes 36

V. The Campus 44

VI. Reflections 96

VII. Alumni of Distinction 130

VIII. Bibliography 139

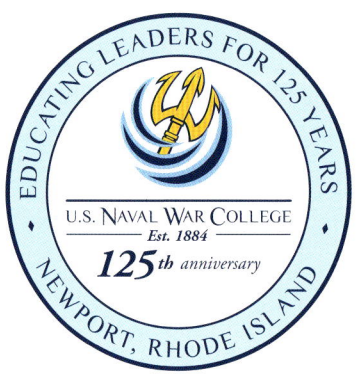

On 6 October 1884, Navy Secretary William E. Chandler issued General Order Number 325 establishing a college "for an advanced course of professional study for naval officers." This was the culminating event in a lengthy series of actions by Commodore Stephen B. Luce and other Navy intellectuals to establish ". . . a place where our officers will not only be encouraged, but required, to study their profession proper—war—in a far more thorough manner than has ever heretofore been attempted, and to bring to the investigation of the various problems of modern naval warfare the scientific methods adopted in other professions."

Though many bureaucratic hurdles remained to be overcome before the concept became reality, the College traces its roots to the 6 October 1884 order. The College began to celebrate its quasquicentennial, or 125th Anniversary, on 6 October 2009 with a series of events leading up to the graduation of the Anniversary Class in June 2010. Planned events include a commemoration of the signing of the General Order, museum exhibits, special lectures and presentations, and the publication of an update to the book *Sailors and Scholars: The Centennial History of the U.S. Naval War College* which is scheduled for a summer 2010 release.

GENERAL ORDER, No. 325.

October 6, 1884.

A college is hereby established for an advanced course of professional study for naval officers, to be known as the Naval War College. It will be under the general supervision of the Bureau of Navigation. The principal building on Coasters' Harbor Island, Newport, R. I., will be assigned to its use, and is hereby transferred, with the surrounding structures and the grounds immediately adjacent, to the custody and control of the Bureau of Navigation for that purpose.

The college will be under the immediate charge of an officer of the Navy, not below the grade of commander, to be known as the President of the Naval War College. He will be assisted in the performance of his duties by a faculty.

A course of instruction, embracing the higher branches of professional study, will be arranged by a board, consisting of all the members of the faculty and including the president, who will be the presiding officer of the board. The board will have regular meetings at least once a month, and at such other times as the president may direct, for the transaction of business. The proceedings of the board will be recorded in a journal.

The course of instruction will be open to all officers above the grade of naval cadet.

Commodore S. B. Luce has been assigned to duty as president of the college.

WM. E. CHANDLER,
Secretary of the Navy.

FROM THE PRESIDENT'S DESK

In Newport Harbor on the 20th of September in 1884, onboard the USS *Tennessee* (1865), the largest American Navy vessel at the time and the flagship of the North Atlantic Squadron, a change of command was held in keeping with Navy custom and tradition. At this ceremony, Commodore Stephen B. Luce, USN, detached from command of the North Atlantic Station and was ordered to go ashore and assume duties as the Superintendent of the College at Coasters Harbor Island. Upon arrival, Commodore Luce put his hand on the door of the sole building on the island and said:

"Know all men by these presents, and in the name of the Father, Son, and Holy Ghost, I christen this building the War College of the American Navy."

Sixteen days later on 6 October 1884, Secretary of the Navy Chandler signed General Order 325, which formally established the Naval War College as "an advanced course of professional study."

From this humble beginning in a building donated by the citizens of Newport, the Naval War College has evolved into one of the premier military education institutions in the world. Over the 125 years the College has been in existence, it has educated tens of thousands of students, hosted dignitaries from U.S. Presidents to moon-walking astronauts, and contributed to the intellectual discourse of the nation in times of peace and in times of conflict. As our anniversary motto declares, through education, research and debate, we have been "Educating Leaders for 125 Years."

In the pages that follow, you will find a brief overview of the College's storied history; you will get a virtual tour of our campus facilities; and you will read testimony on the value of a Naval War College education from some of its most distinguished alumni. I hope you will find this information as informative and interesting as I did.

I am indeed honored to be serving as the 52nd President of the Naval War College during our 125th anniversary year. All of us at the College are the inheritors of a marvelous legacy of excellence created by our predecessors over more than a dozen decades. We look forward to a future that is equally bright.

J. P. WISECUP
Rear Admiral, U.S. Navy

"As leaders, it is incumbent upon us to carefully consider the future for our Sailors, our Navy and our nation. As you become more senior and take on more responsibility, it is increasingly important, and more challenging, to make and take time to think. The Naval War College is a place for men and women from all services to do just that. Taking the time to think, especially at rigorous institutions such as the Naval War College, and making it a habit, will pay off greatly for you and our Navy."

GARY ROUGHEAD
Admiral, U.S. Navy
Chief of Naval Operations
6 April 2008

State of Rhode Island and Providence Plantations

GUBERNATORIAL PROCLAMATION

Whereas, for 125 years the United States Naval War College has been educating future military and civilian leaders, and conducting state-of-the-art conflict simulation and original research on national security issues; and

Whereas, the College's International Education and Outreach Programs have promoted trust and confidence with allied military services around the globe; and

Whereas, Naval War College alumni have contributed significantly to victory in the nation's military conflicts, and to the avoidance of war and the preservation of peace in times of crisis; and

Whereas, the College today is educating over 30,000 men and women on its Newport campus, around the nation through its Fleet Seminars, and around the world through its internet-based courses; and

Whereas, the College's faculty, staff and student body have served as marvelous neighbors and friends who have learned from, and enriched, the lives of the citizens of the entire New England Region;

NOW, THEREFORE, I, DONALD L. CARCIERI, GOVERNOR OF THE STATE OF RHODE ISLAND AND PROVIDENCE PLANTATIONS, DO HEREBY PROCLAIM,

October 6, 2009
as
Naval War College Day

in the State of Rhode Island and encourage all of its citizens to join in recognizing the importance of the Naval War College to the state and the nation.

In recognition whereof, I have hereby set my hand and caused the Seal of the State of Rhode Island and Providence Plantations to be hereunto affixed this 6th day of October 2009.

Donald L. Carcieri
Governor

A. Ralph Mollis
Secretary of State

Congressional Record

PROCEEDINGS AND DEBATES OF THE 111th CONGRESS, FIRST SESSION

Vol. 155   WASHINGTON, TUESDAY, OCTOBER 6, 2009   *No. 143*

Senate

125TH ANNIVERSARY OF THE U.S. NAVAL WAR COLLEGE

Mr. REED. Mr. President, today I recognize the 125th anniversary of the U.S. Naval War College. The Naval War College was established on October 6, 1884, in Newport, RI, to provide an advanced course of professional study for both military officers and civilians. The mission has evolved over the years to include developing strategic and operational leaders, helping the Chief of Naval Operations define the future Navy, strengthening maritime security cooperation, and supporting combat readiness.

The Naval War College serves as a center for research that develops advanced strategic, war fighting, and campaign concepts for future deployment of maritime, joint, and combined forces. The Naval War College works closely with the Navy Warfare Development Command and the Chief of Naval Operations Strategic Studies Group in developing and analyzing national security issues. Through the Naval Command College and the Naval Staff College, naval officers from around the world come to prepare for high command responsibilities, and to learn about the U.S. Navy's methods, practice, and doctrine. The Naval War College also supports combat readiness among the U.S. Navy's commanders through operational planning, analysis, and war-gaming to respond to changing operational environments.

Some of our Nation's greatest military and civilian leaders have attended the Naval War College including FADM Chester Nimitz, the Commander of the Pacific Fleet during World War II; RADM Alan Shepard, the first American in space; Ambassador Christopher Hill, the current U.S. Ambassador to Iraq; and Marine Corps GEN James Cartwright, the current Vice Chairman of the Joint Chiefs of Staff. Indeed, even our two combatant commanders in Afghanistan and Iraq, GEN Stanley McChrystal and GEN Raymond Odierno, are both graduates of the Naval War College.

I am proud of the talented men and women who have made the Naval War College the strong institution it is today, and I congratulate the entire Naval War College community on this important milestone.

Jack Reed
US Senator, RI

Introduction

The Naval War College is the leading institution of its kind in the world. More than a century ago, its founder succinctly defined its purpose and meaning "as a place of original research on all questions relating to war and to statesmanship connected with war, or the prevention of war." The College has repeatedly been in the forefront of national and international thinking about the nature and character of naval warfare and the strategic and operational roles of navies in both war and peace. Over the decades in preparation for potential conflict, numerous uniformed leaders have gathered in Newport to study and to reflect on all the most difficult political and military analytical issues that nations face on the world's oceans, knowing that once a crisis breaks it is too late to do such preparatory analysis and thinking. In this, the College provides a unique place where it strives to develop critical thinking and be a place where current and future leaders in uniform have an opportunity to look beyond their normal structured military tasks and to think about, talk, develop, and debate the highest professional issues with their colleagues, their counterparts in other services and from other nations as well as with some of the best thinkers and academicians available. The greatest challenge to the Naval War College is to continue to build and to maintain its intellectual integrity where such interactions can take place in an educational setting that will provide leaders with the intellectual depth that can serve the nation in peace and war at the highest levels of responsibility.

The first fruit of the College's contributions came in 1890 with the world-famous historical and strategic analyses of Alfred Thayer Mahan about *The Influence of Sea Power Upon History*. The books he wrote for the Naval War College earned him plaudits around the world. In response to the world's praise, he was careful to point out that the reason he was able to develop a new and systematic approach to the problems of naval warfare was not due to his personal qualities, but as he wrote, "due, wholly, and exclusively, to the Naval War College, which was instituted to promote such studies."

Since its founding in 1884, the College has produced thousands of graduates from its residence programs. Alumni have gone on to serve their nations with the greatest distinction in both war and peace. When the United States entered World War II, every Admiral less one qualified to command at sea, Nimitz, Halsey, Spruance and King among them, was a graduate of the Naval War College. These officers played major roles in the success of U.S. naval operations during the war. Additionally, fifteen graduates earned the Congressional Medal of Honor. Service at the highest level of the military has continued to be a hallmark of the Naval War College graduates.

Over the past two decades, Naval War College alumni served as the Chairman of the Joint Chiefs of Staff, Commandant of the Coast Guard, Vice Chief of Naval Operations, Commander-in-Chief Pacific, and Ambassador to the People's Republic of China. In addition to these officers wearing all of the different American service uniforms, the College has also educated officers from other navies. Since its programs for international officers first began half a century ago in 1956, the College has educated over 3,400 naval officers from 129 different navies. Of the over 1,700 graduates of the senior-level Naval Command College, 866 have become flag officers and 200 have become chiefs of their navies, of which thirteen are currently in office. Of the over 1,700 graduates of the younger, intermediate-level Naval Staff College, 272 have become flag officers and 97 have risen to be service chiefs, with twenty-two of them currently in office. Moreover, two Naval Command College graduates have become presidents of their nations.

HISTORY

Above: Dewey Field with USS *Iowa* in background in 2001. U.S. Navy Photo.

"My year as a student at the Naval Command and Staff course was a professional career highlight. This rich educational opportunity expanded my understanding of strategic issues and National Security policy. The curriculum also exposed us to decision making in an atmosphere of uncertainty and I learned the essentiality of good data and rigorous analysis in the pursuit of alternatives. The Naval War College experience was a profoundly positive influence on my professional and personal development."

Admiral William J. Fallon, U.S. Navy
Former Commander, U.S. Central Command

The Naval War College (NWC) is a combination of buildings used since the founding of the Navy's premier academic institution in 1884. Founders Hall, now the home of the NWC Museum, was the first building in use on 6 October 1884 when the War College was established by the Secretary of the Navy, William E. Chandler. Founders Hall served as the "poor house" for the city of Newport before it was donated to the Navy. The Naval War College is the oldest institution of its kind in continuous existence in the world today. There are four resident colleges with more than 600 students currently attending the College. The student body consists of U.S. military officers from all branches of the armed forces, career civilians from a variety of federal government agencies and international naval officers.

As the Naval War College entered the 20th century it faced a very uncertain future. Many U.S. naval officers had an ingrained belief that everything an officer needed to know could be learned on a ship. By May 1917, the College had become both a laboratory and a war planning agency for the Navy Department. Almost every war plan adopted between 1890 and 1917 was prepared by NWC officers alone or in joint effort with the Office of Naval Intelligence.

In 1956, the Naval Command College was established as a study for senior international officers. The 1960s brought about the establishment of two separate courses for U.S military officers and civilian federal career employees, the College of Naval Command & Staff and the College of Naval Warfare. Noting a need to educate mid-grade international officers, the Naval War College established in 1972 the Naval Staff College. In 1981, the Chief of Naval Operations expressed concern over specific avenues of study and how they were addressed by the Naval War College. This prompted the development of the Center for Naval Warfare Studies and the CNO's Strategic Studies Group to conduct original research concerning strategic options for the future. This group in turn reports its findings directly to the CNO.

In 1991, the New England Association of Schools and Colleges accredited the Naval War College to award a Master of Arts degree in National Security & Strategic Studies to qualified graduates of the two U.S. colleges. In 2007, senior students began to receive Joint Professional Military Education Level I and II certification upon graduation.

HISTORY

NAVAL WAR COLLEGE OPENED.

Assistant Secretary of the Navy Roosevelt Appeals for a Great Navy.

NEWPORT, June 2.—The Naval War College was formally opened to-day with an address by Theodore Roosevelt, Assistant Secretary of the Navy. The address was delivered in the lecture room of the college. Among those present were Commodore Wallace and officers of the naval station, Col. Pennington, commander of Fort Adams, and Commander McGowan of the naval training station.

Commander C. F. Goodrich, President of the War College, introduced Mr. Roosevelt. Mr. Roosevelt's address was entitled "Washington's Forgotten Maxim, Namely, 'To be Prepared for War Is the Most Effectual Means to Promote Peace.'" The burden of Mr. Roosevelt's remarks was that while torpedo boats and cruisers were useful, the possession by the United States of twenty battleships would make war altogether unlikely. Among other things he said:

"If we forget that in the last resort we can only secure peace by being ready and willing to fight for it, we may some day have bitter cause to realize that a rich nation, which is slothful, timid, or unwieldy is an easy prey for any people which still retains those most valuable of all qualities, the soldierly virtues.

"Merely for the protection of our own shores we need a great navy, and what is more, we need it to protect our interests in the islands from which it is possible to command our shores and to protect our commerce on the high seas.

"I believe with all my heart in the Monroe doctrine, and I believe also that the great mass of the American people are loyal to it; but it is worse than idle to announce our adherence to this doctrine and yet to decline to take measures to show that ours is not mere lip loyalty.

"If we possess a formidable navy, small is the chance indeed that we shall ever be dragged into a war to uphold the Monroe doctrine. If we do not possess such a navy, war may be forced upon us at any time.

"We ask for a great navy, partly because we think that the possession of such a navy is the surest guarantee of peace, and partly because we feel that no National life is worth having if the Nation is not willing, when the need shall arise, to stake everything on the supreme arbitrament of war, and to pour out its blood, its treasure, and tears like water, rather than submit to the loss of honor and renown.

"We ask for a great navy, we ask for an armament fit for the Nation's needs, not primarily to fight, but to avert fighting. Preparedness deters the foe, and maintains right by the show of ready might without the use of violence. Peace, like freedom, is not a gift that tarries long in the hands of cowards, or of those too feeble or too short-sighted to deserve it, and we ask to be given the means to insure that honorable peace which is alone worth having."

Above: Photo of the print *The Continental Sloop "Providence." The Navy and History of Rhode Island.*

Ever since the Italian navigator Giovanni Verrazzano first sailed into Narragansett Bay in 1524, Rhode Island has always been associated with access to and from the sea. In 1775, Rhode Island founded the first state Navy, the Rhode Island State Navy, and was the first state to advocate the formation of a Continental Navy. The most notable ship in Rhode Island's navy was the *Katy*, formerly a merchant sloop. The *Katy* was eventually re-commissioned as the *Providence* and commanded by John Paul Jones of the Continental Navy. In spite of the patriots' attempts to protect Narragansett Bay, the British occupied Newport from 1776 to 1779, effectively creating a blockade at the entrance to the bay.

In 1778, the Continental Army attempted to re-take Newport, a failed campaign known as the Battle of Rhode Island. After the war, many Newport families continued to serve in the Navy, most notably, the Perry family: Oliver Hazard Perry of War of 1812 fame, and his brother, Matthew Calbraith Perry. In 1852, Matthew Perry commanded a naval expedition to Japan, which resulted in a treaty with the United States. Today, the City of Newport continues to remember Matthew Perry with its annual Black Ships Festival, a Japanese cultural celebration. Both Oliver Hazard and Matthew Perry are buried in Newport's Island Cemetery.

Left: Picture of Giovanni Verrazzano. *The Navy and History of Rhode Island.*

Opposite: Bay of Narragansett by C. Blaskowitz. This version of the map is most important because it was issued during the Revolution and was published in London by William Faden in 1777.

Coasters Harbor Island, located two miles north of the center of Newport and since 1883 home to a portion of the U.S. Navy in the Narragansett Bay region, is where the founders of the City-by-the-Sea first landed in 1639. The incident occurred on 30 April and was recorded years later by Peter Easton, son of Nicholas Easton, formerly of Portsmouth, Rhode Island (1638) and one of the principals in the Newport settlement project. Writing in the margin of a page for the year 1639 in his copy of Nathaniel Morton's *New England Memorial* (Cambridge, Massachusetts, 1669) Easton noted:

"In the beginning of May this year the Eastons came to Newport in Road Iland and builded ther the first English building and ther planted this year and coming by boat they lodged at the Iland called coasters harbour the last of April 1639 and the First of May in the morning gave the Iland the name Coasters Harbour and from thence came to Newport the same Day."

On 30 April 1924, two hundred and eighty-five years later, the Naval Training Station commemorated the historic event by the dedication of a monument in front of its administration building, now Founders Hall of the Naval War College and home to the College museum. Popularly known as the Settler's Stone, it consists of a large oval-shaped boulder to which is affixed a bronze plaque containing an enlargement of Peter Easton's original descriptive narrative.

The Easton document, which, incidentally, is in the Easton Family Papers in the American Antiquarian Society, Worcester, Massachusetts, is highly significant to the early history of the region in that it reveals how Coasters Harbor Island got its name and precisely when Newport was founded, namely, the first of May.

The landing of the Eastons on the island on the last day of April 1639 did not signal the beginnings of Newport. On the contrary, the town was limited to the Aquidneck Island site. The off-shore islands, Coasters Harbor Island and Goat Island, were not included. In fact, Weenat Shassit and Nantee Sinuck, as the two islands were called by their Indian owners, did not become part of Newport until 1673. Benedict Arnold and John Greene had purchased them in 1658, supposedly on behalf of the town, but transfer of deed did not occur until fifteen years later.

Coasters Harbor Island remained town property for over two hundred years, until 1881, when it was ceded to the United States for use as a naval training station. The federal government officially accepted the gift the following year and in June 1883, it became the site of the Newport Naval Training Station, the first shore-based recruit training activity in America.

An interesting feature of the 1924 Naval Station commemoration was the burying of a time capsule under the Settler's Stone. This occurred several days before the dedication ceremonies and with Station Commander, Captain Franck T. Evans, and representatives of the Newport Historical Society present.

The original plans called for the stone to be set in a cement base located just below ground level. When the idea of a time capsule was subsequently approved, however, the need for a more substantial base became apparent. Accordingly, a hole was dug measuring 6 feet deep by 6 feet long by 4 feet wide and then filled to a half-way mark with cement. At this point, a wooden box containing a large wax-sealed bottle holding Naval Training Station and Newport city memorabilia, chiefly 1923–24 imprints and photographs, was placed in the center. The pouring was then resumed, and when the wet mass approached ground level, the Settler's Stone was partially immersed and held in place until the cement was completely dry. Consequently, the Coasters Harbor Island time capsule is at the very heart of the large concrete block.

Right: The Settler's Stone, 2008. Photo by JD DuVall.

History

Founders Hall

In 1820, the Newport Overseers of the Poor chose to build the new Newport Asylum for the Poor on Coasters Harbor Island, an uninhabited island off the coast of Newport that had served as a quarantine station in the eighteenth century. Constructed of island fieldstone, the building was completed in 1822. Unable to leave the island without the permission of the caretaker, asylum inmates (abject poor, the lame, the blind, and the insane) were expected to work for their room and board, either in the house or adjoining farm.

A short walk around Founders Hall there is a small cemetery on the east side of slope where six Newport residents are buried from the mid- to late 1700s era.

The asylum continued in operation until 1883, when the U.S. Navy acquired Coasters Harbor Island for the purpose of establishing a training school for seamen. When Commodore Stephen B. Luce proposed that the Navy also establish a college for naval officers in 1884—the Naval War College—this building served as its first home, with students studying and living within its halls. It is the place where Alfred Thayer Mahan gave his famous lectures that became his book, "Influence of Sea Power Upon History 1660–1783." It is for this reason that this structure has been renamed Founders Hall. It is now listed on the National Register of Historic Landmarks.

From 1894 to 1977, the United States Marine Corps guarded the halls of the College. A bronze plaque located in Spruance Lobby commemorates their dedication.

Above: Founders Hall in the background, 1890. Naval War College Museum.

PRESIDENTS

"Next to actual experience afloat, the Naval War College is the most important factor in our training of captains and admirals."

Rear Admiral Caspar F. Goodrich, U.S. Navy
Address to the 43rd Convention of the
National Educational Association
June 30, 1904

Inset: Rear Admiral Goodrich. Portrait photograph by Harris & Ewing, Washington, D.C., taken circa 1904–1909. (NH 49353)

View of Newport Naval Station Marina, 2003. U.S. Navy Photo.

Presidents of the Naval War College 1884–1939

The following list assigns numbers to each President of the Naval War College, but does not give a number for officers who served as Acting President. The names of Acting Presidents are given only when they fill a gap between permanent appointments as President. Officers who served as President in two or more separate and distinct assignments are given a number for each assignment.

	Rank	Name	From	To
1.	Commodore	Stephen Bleecker Luce	Oct 6, 1884	June 22, 1886
2.	Captain	Alfred Thayer Mahan	June 22, 1886	Jan 12, 1889
3.	Commander	Casper Frederick Goodrich	Jan 12, 1889	July 22, 1892
4.	Captain	Alfred Thayer Mahan	July 22, 1892	May 10, 1893
5.	Commander	Charles Herbert Stockton	May 10, 1893	Nov 13, 1893
6.	Commander	Henry Clay Taylor	Nov 15, 1893	Dec 31, 1896
7.	Captain	Casper Frederick Goodrich	Dec 31, 1896	Apr 23, 1898

Note: During the period from March 22, 1898 to November 2, 1898, the activities of the War College were discontinued on account of the participation of the United States in the Spanish-American War.

	Rank	Name	From	To
8.	Captain	Charles Herbert Stockton	Nov 2, 1898	Oct 25, 1900
9.	Rear Admiral	French Ensor Chadwick	Oct 25, 1900	Nov 16, 1903
10.	Captain	Charles Stillman Sperry	Nov 16, 1903	May 24, 1906
11.	Rear Admiral	John Porter Merrell	May 24, 1906	Oct 6, 1909
12.	Rear Admiral	Raymond Perry Rodgers	Oct 6, 1909	Nov 20, 1911
13.	Captain	William Ledyard Rodgers	Nov 20, 1911	Dec 15, 1913
14.	Rear Admiral	Austin Melvin Knight	Dec 15, 1913	Feb 16, 1917
15.	Captain	William Sowden Sims	Feb 16, 1917	Apr 28, 1917

Note: During the period from April 28, 1917 to April 11, 1919, the academic activities of the War College were discontinued on account of the participation of the United States in the World War. During this period, the reserve force of the Second Naval District used the College buildings and a series of three Acting Presidents maintained the administrative side of the College.

	Rank	Name	From	To
	Commander	Charles P. Eaton (Ret.) (Acting)	May 1, 1917	Nov 21, 1917
	Commodore	James Parker (Ret.) (Acting)	Nov 21, 1917	Mar 17, 1919
	Captain	Reginald R. Belknap (Acting)	Mar 17, 1919	Apr 11, 1919
16.	Rear Admiral	William Sowden Sims	Apr 11, 1919	Oct 14, 1922
	Captain	D. Blamer (Acting)	Oct 14, 1922	Nov 3, 1922
17.	Rear Admiral	Clarence Stewart Williams	Nov 3, 1922	Sept 5, 1925
18.	Rear Admiral	William Veazie Pratt	Sept 5, 1925	Sept 17, 1927
19.	Rear Admiral	Joel Roberts Poinsett Pringle	Sept 19, 1927	May 30, 1930
	Captain	S.W. Bryant (Acting)	May 30, 1930	June 16, 1930
20.	Rear Admiral	Harris Laning	June 16, 1930	May 13, 1933
	Captain	Adolphus Andrews (Acting)	May 13, 1933	June 3, 1933
21.	Rear Admiral	Luke McNamee	June 3, 1933	May 29, 1934
	Captain	H.D. Cooke (Acting)	May 29, 1934	June 18, 1934
22.	Rear Admiral	Edward Clifford Kalbfus	June 18, 1934	Dec 15, 1936
	Captain	H.D. Cooke (Acting)	Dec 15, 1936	Jan 2, 1936
23.	Rear Admiral	Charles Philip Snyder	Jan 2, 1937	May 27, 1939
	Captain	J.W. Wilcox (Acting)	May 27, 1939	June 30, 1939

Presidents of the Naval War College 1939–2009

	Rank	Name	From	To
24.	Rear Admiral	Edward Clifford Kalbfus	June 30, 1939	June 16, 1942
	Admiral	Edward Clifford Kalbfus (Ret.)	June 16, 1942	Nov 2, 1942
25.	Rear Admiral	William Satterlee Pye	Nov 2, 1942	July 1, 1944
	Vice Admiral	William Satterlee Pye (Ret.)	July 1, 1944	Mar 1, 1946
26.	Admiral	Raymond Ames Spruance	Mar 1, 1946	July 1, 1948
	Rear Admiral	Allen Edward Smith (Acting)	July 1, 1948	Nov 1, 1948
27.	Vice Admiral	Donald Bradford Beary	Nov 1, 1948	May 28, 1950
	Rear Admiral	Thomas Ross Cooley (Acting)	May 28, 1950	Oct 17, 1950
	Captain	Harry D. Felt (Acting)	Oct 17, 1950	Dec 1, 1950
28.	Vice Admiral	Richard L. Conolly	Dec 1, 1950	Nov 2, 1953
	Rear Admiral	Thomas H. Robbins, Jr. (Acting)	Nov 2, 1953	May 3, 1954
29.	Vice Admiral	Lynde D. McCormick	May 3, 1954	Aug 16, 1956
	Rear Admiral	Thomas H. Robbins, Jr. (Acting)	Aug 16, 1956	Sept 4, 1956
30.	Rear Admiral	Thomas H. Robbins, Jr.	Sept 5, 1956	Aug 1, 1957
31.	Vice Admiral	Stuart H. Ingersoll	Aug 13, 1957	June 30, 1960
32.	Vice Admiral	Bernard L. Austin	June 30, 1960	July 31, 1964
33.	Vice Admiral	Charles L. Melson	July 31, 1964	Jan 25, 1966
	Rear Admiral	Francis E. Nuessle (Acting)	Jan 25, 1966	Feb 15, 1966
34.	Vice Admiral	John T. Hayward	Feb 15, 1966	Aug 30, 1968
35.	Vice Admiral	Richard G. Colbert	Aug 30, 1968	Aug 17, 1971
36.	Vice Admiral	Benedict J. Semmes, Jr.	Aug 17, 1971	June 30, 1972
37.	Vice Admiral	Stansfield Turner	June 30, 1972	Aug 9, 1974
38.	Vice Admiral	Julien J. Le Bourgeois	Aug 9, 1974	Apr 1, 1977
39.	Rear Admiral	Huntington Hardisty	Apr 1, 1977	Oct 13, 1977
40.	Vice Admiral	James B. Stockdale	Oct 13, 1977	Aug 22, 1979
41.	Rear Admiral	Edward F. Welch, Jr.	Aug 22, 1979	Aug 17, 1982
	Captain	David Self (Acting)	Aug 18, 1982	Oct 14, 1982
42.	Rear Admiral	James E. Service	Oct 14, 1982	July 12, 1985
	Captain	Robert Watts (Acting)	July 12, 1985	Aug 8, 1985
43.	Rear Admiral	Ronald F. Marryott	Aug 8, 1985	Aug 12, 1986
	Captain	Robert Watts (Acting)	Aug 12, 1986	Sept 2, 1986
44.	Rear Admiral	John A. Baldwin	Sept 2, 1986	Aug 11, 1987
45.	Rear Admiral	Ronald J. Kurth	Aug 11, 1987	July 17, 1990
46.	Rear Admiral	Joseph C. Strasser	July 17, 1990	June 29, 1995
47.	Rear Admiral	James R. Stark	June 29, 1995	July 24, 1998
48.	Vice Admiral	Arthur K. Cebrowski	July 24, 1998	Aug 22, 2001
49.	Rear Admiral	Rodney P. Rempt	Aug 22, 2001	July 9, 2003
50.	Rear Admiral	Ronald A. Route	July 9, 2003	Aug 12, 2004
51.	Rear Admiral	Jacob L. Shuford	Aug 12, 2004	Nov 6, 2008
52.	Rear Admiral	James P. Wisecup	Nov 6, 2008	Present

Extracted from the United States Naval War College Register of Officers (1884–1970); *Sailors and Scholars* by Hattendorf, Simpson, and Wadleigh (1970–1984); and Naval War College Museum (1984–present).

Rear Admiral Stephen B. Luce
October 6, 1884–June 22, 1886

In 1884, Rear Admiral Luce founded the Naval War College. He was the leader of a movement for naval professionalism and modernization in the last half of the 19th century. His earlier accomplishments in these regards included: publication of the first Naval Academy textbook on seamanship, 1862; charter membership in the United States Naval Institution, 1873; founder of the first state maritime school, 1874; founder of the Naval Apprentice System for training recruits afloat, 1875; founder of the first shore-based naval recruit training station at Newport, Rhode Island, 1880–1883. Luce served as the Naval War College's first President, 1884–1886, and he remained in close association with the school until his death in 1917.

Painting of Rear Admiral Stephen B. Luce by Frederic Vinton, 1900. Oil, framed, 60 x 40. Commissioned by the Naval War College.

Rear Admiral Alfred Thayer Mahan
June 22, 1886–January 12, 1889
July 22, 1892–May 10, 1893

Rear Admiral Mahan was a key instrumental figure during the first few years of the Naval War College. He not only was the President, but he also was a key lecturer. He lectured in naval strategy and tactics focused on the interrelationships among naval and military tactics, strategy, diplomacy, and national power. His lectures and work resulted in his famous book, *The Influence of Sea Power Upon History, 1660–1783*. During his tenure he and William McCarty Little began war-gaming. They devised a unique system to examine and explain historic battle tactics by using cardboard vessels and drawing paper. During his presidency the Naval War College was threatened with closure. Secretary Herbert took a trip to Newport to shut down the school. During his trip he read Mahan's book *The Influence of Sea Power Upon the French Revolution*. After reading this book Herbert stated, "When I embarked on this cruise, I had fully intended to abolish the college; I now intend to do all in my power to sustain it." The work of Mahan was both the result and the savior of the College and its first decade.

Painting of Rear Admiral Alfred T. Mahan by Alexander James, 1945. Oil, framed, 41 x 54. Commissioned by the naval officers under Admiral W.S. Pye.

Rear Admiral Caspar F. Goodrich
January 12, 1889–July 22, 1892
December 31, 1896–April 23, 1898

During Rear Admiral Goodrich's tenure the College was on the verge of being shut down. He had to defend the importance of the Naval War College. He wrote to show the virtues of education that "the information obtained from one single strategic game in three hours could not be secured by the north Atlantic Fleet in as many weeks." Shortly after his tenure started, the Spanish-American War broke out and thus he was ordered to command the USS *St. Louis*. The Naval War College suspended its courses until the end of the war.

Painting of Rear Admiral Caspar F. Goodrich by Paul Thonry. Oil, framed, 49 x 33. Gift of Mrs. Ross Jones to the Naval War College.

Rear Admiral Charles S. Sperry
November 16, 1903–May 24, 1906

Rear Admiral Sperry went to the Naval Academy during the Civil War in 1862, while the academy was located at Newport, Rhode Island. In 1866, he graduated tenth in his class. He served as President of the Naval War College from 1903–1906. During his tenure at the War College, he developed an extensive knowledge of international law. His first flag assignment was as a delegate to the International Conference to Review Rules for Treatment of Sick and Wounded in Geneva. The following year, he was a delegate to the Second Hague Conference on Prize Law. At the end of the Hague Conference, the Navy Department ordered Sperry to assume command of the 4th Division, United States Atlantic Fleet, just in time to take part in the world cruise of the "Great White Fleet." Starting in May 1908, Sperry commanded the Great White Fleet.

Painting of Rear Admiral Charles S. Sperry by Sergeant Kendall, 1911. Oil, framed, 55 x 35. Gift of Admiral Sperry.

Rear Admiral William Sowden Sims
February 16, 1917–April 28, 1917
April 11, 1919–October 14, 1922

One of the great reformers in naval gunfire and employment of destroyer ships. Commander of U.S. Naval Forces in European waters during World War I, he adopted the use of naval convoys and promoted the construction of destroyers to counter Germany's use of unrestricted submarine warfare. He served as President of the Naval War College in 1917 and from 1919 to 1922. His book on Anglo-American naval cooperation in the war at sea during World War I, *Victory at Sea,* won the Pulitzer Prize in history in 1920.

Painting of Rear Admiral William S. Sims by unknown artist. Oil, framed, 72 x 35. Gift of Mrs. Williams S. Sims to the Naval War College.

Admiral William V. Pratt
September 5, 1925–September 17, 1927

Admiral William V. Pratt had served as a member of the Naval War College staff in 1911–1912. Once becoming College President in 1925, he instituted reforms that changed the focus of reforming student education significantly for the future. Most importantly, he believed that naval officers should be made to view the totality of modern warfare, and he expanded course requirements to include much more than tactics and strategy. Pratt rose to the rank of Admiral and was the first President of the Naval War College to hold the office of Chief of Naval Operations, serving in that capacity from September 1930 up through June 1933.

Painting of Admiral William V. Pratt by C. S. Slade. Oil, framed, 36 x 42. Gift of William Veazie Pratt, Jr. to the Naval War College.

Vice Admiral Joel P. Pringle
September 19, 1927–May 30, 1930

Vice Admiral Pringle was instrumental in construction of what is now called Pringle Hall.

The nineteenth President of the College, Joel R. P. Pringle (1873–1932), had been the first commanding officer of the destroyer USS *Perkins* (D 26) in 1910 and went on to command the destroyer tender USS *Dixie* (AD 1), Flotilla 2 of the Destroyer Force, Atlantic Fleet, and the battleship USS *Idaho* (BB 24). During World War One, he was simultaneously Chief of Staff, Destroyer Flotilla, European Waters, and Commanding Officer of the destroyer tender USS *Melville* (AD 2), Admiral Sims's flagship. He graduated from the Naval War College in 1920 and served as Chief of Staff at the Naval War College in 1923–1925 under Rear Admiral C. S. Williams. As a flag officer at sea, he commanded Battleship Division 3 in the Battle Force and was later Commander, Battleships, Battle Force.

Painting of Vice Admiral Joel P. Pringle by C. Hopkinson, 1936. Oil, framed, 72 x 34. Commissioned by friends of Admiral Pringle.

Admiral Edward C. Kalbfus
June 18, 1934–December 15, 1936
June 30, 1939–November 2, 1942

A staunch believer in the value of the Naval War College to the service, Admiral Edward C. Kalbfus exerted strenuous efforts to forward the institution's objectives and to enhance its status within the Naval Department. He graduated from the College in 1927, served two years on the staff and served two separate tours as President. He is best remembered for the production by the College of *Sound Military Decision* (1942), the only published guide for naval planning in the Navy, and for the successful efforts that he made to keep the College open during the Second World War.

Painting of Admiral Kalbfus by Albert Murray, ca. 1945. Oil, framed, 44 x 44. On loan from the Navy Art Collection.

Vice Admiral William S. Pye
November 2, 1942–March 1, 1946

Vice Admiral Pye's association with the Naval War College dates back to the years just prior to the First World War when he served as a member of the staff. He was at the College again in 1934–1935 as a member of the first Advanced Class. Keenly interested in the school and in the development of naval education, Pye remained in close association, eventually becoming College President during the Second World War.

Painting of Vice Admiral William S. Pye by Stanislaus Rembski, 1943. Oil, framed, 45 x 39. Gift of Mrs. W. S. Pye to the Naval War College.

Admiral Raymond Ames Spruance
March 1, 1946–July 1, 1948

In 1927, Admiral Spruance graduated from the Naval War College. He then served on the Naval War College faculty in 1931–1933 and then again in 1935–1938. He was promoted to Rear Admiral in 1940. His first flag assignment was as Commandant of the Tenth Naval District at San Juan, Puerto Rico. In 1946–1948, Spruance served as the President of the Naval War College. Both a product of and a firm believer in the importance of the professional military education that the Naval War College provided for mid-career officers, Spruance did everything possible to improve the College's circumstances during his administration as the College's President. He established new and innovative changes in the College's administration and curriculum. Among his major achievements were to create departments to teach operational logistics, to analyze and to plan to establish a civilian faculty for the College, beginning with his recommendation to start with an academic chair to be occupied by a scholar of the history of sea power. In addition, he laid the groundwork for what would eventually become the *Naval War College Review*.

Painting of Admiral Raymond Ames Spruance by George Sottung, 1983. Oil, framed. Acquired through the Naval War College Foundation.

Vice Admiral Donald B. Beary
November 1, 1948–May 28, 1950

Donald B. Beary (1888–1966) was awarded the Navy Cross for convoy duty in World War One. When the United States entered World War Two in 1941, Beary commanded the Fleet Operational Training Command, Atlantic. Later, during the battles of Iwo Jima and Okinawa in 1944, he was serving as Commander, Service Squadron 6, and was assigned the task of providing at-sea support to the Third and Fifth Fleets. At the Naval War College, Vice Admiral Beary undertook to broaden the students' views by bringing to Newport a wide variety of business authorities and leaders to meet and have discussions with students. What were first referred to as round-table discussions blossomed into the Global Strategy Discussions of the 1950s and, eventually, into the present-day Current Strategy Forum. The *Knox*-class frigate USS *Donald B. Beary* (FF 1085) was named for him.

Painting of Vice Admiral Donald B. Beary by John Capolino, 1950. Oil, framed, 31 x 37. Commissioned by the Naval War College.

Vice Admiral Richard L. Conolly
December 1, 1950–November 2, 1953

As a Lieutenant Commander, Richard Lansing Conolly (1892–1962) graduated from the Naval War College in 1931 and then went on for a year to teach strategy and tactics on the College's faculty. In 1942–1943, Conolly was assistant planning officer on the staff of Admiral Ernest J. King and planned the invasion of Guadalcanal and North Africa. In 1943, he served as Commander of Landing Craft and Bases during the invasions of North Africa and Italy, then commanded the Amphibious Assault Group at Kwajalein in 1944. His most famous assault was the successful recapture of Guam in July 1944. One historian has written of him, "To the US Marines, Conolly was the most admired naval officer to emerge from the Pacific theater." After the war he was promoted to four stars as Commander in Chief, U.S. Naval Forces, Europe, Eastern Atlantic, and Mediterranean (CINCNELM). As the twenty-eighth President of the Naval War College, Conolly reverted to three-star rank and made substantial and important reforms to build on the insights gained during World War Two, including reviving Admiral Spruance's recommendation to create visiting civilian faculty positions in history and political science. The *Spruance*-class destroyer USS *Conolly* (DD 979) is named for him.

Painting of Vice Admiral Richard L. Conolly by Dwight Shepler, 1952. Oil on canvas. Purchased by the Naval War College.

Vice Admiral Lynde D. McCormick
May 3, 1954–August 16, 1956

Vice Admiral Lynde D. McCormick graduated from the Naval War College in 1938 and went on to a very distinguished career serving for a time as Vice Chief of Naval Operations (1949) and Acting Chief of Naval Operations (1951). He was Commander-in-Charge Atlantic Fleet and Atlantic Command—in which position he also became the first Supreme Allied Commander, Atlantic. In 1956, the second year of his presidency, Admiral McCormick established a new course for senior officers from other navies, the present-day Naval Command College. Regrettably, however, he died shortly thereafter, the first College President to die in office, and the inauguration of the course was left for his successor.

Painting of Admiral Lynde D. McCormick by Edmond Fitzgerald. Oil, framed, 38 x 31. Commissioned by the Naval War College.

Rear Admiral Thomas H. Robbins, Jr.
September 5, 1956–August 1, 1957

Rear Admiral Thomas H. Robbins had many years of service with the Naval War College before becoming President in September 1956. He was a member of the graduating Class of 1937, served on the staff 1938–1939, was acting President during 1953–1954 and Chief of Staff in 1955 and 1956. Robbins inaugurated the senior foreign officer course, later the Naval Command College, in 1957 and when he left the College in August of that year, he became Commandant of the Potomac River Naval Command—making him the first President since the Second World War who did not immediately leave active service.

Painting of Rear Admiral Thomas H. Robbins by Tony Sarro. Oil, framed, 36 x 43. Gift of Mrs. Robbins to the Naval War College.

Vice Admiral Stuart H. Ingersoll
August 13, 1957–June 30, 1960

Vice Admiral Stuart H. Ingersoll became President of the College in August 1957. He had served for twelve years a flag officer and brought to the College a broad background in planning and leadership in postwar unified commands. It was during Ingersoll's administration that war-gaming at the College made a significant change from a manual procedure to computerized. On November 7, 1958 the Naval Electronic Warfare Simulator (NEWS) was commissioned in the central wings of Sims Hall.

Painting of Vice Admiral Stuart H. Ingersoll by Edmond Fitzgerald. Oil, framed, 36 x 30. Commissioned by the Naval War College.

Vice Admiral Bernard L. Austin
June 30, 1960–July 31, 1964

Vice Admiral Bernard L. Austin, the College's twenty-seventh President, remained in office for four years, the longest tour in College history up to that time. Austin came to the College with impeccable credentials in naval warfare. In the Second World War he served as a destroyer captain's squadron commander and sailed with Arleigh Burke's "Little Beaver" squadron in the Solomon Islands Campaign. Subsequently, he joined the staff of Admiral Chester W. Nimitz, Commander Pacific Fleet, becoming the youngest flag officer in the Navy when he was spot-promoted Commodore.

Painting of Vice Admiral Bernard L. Austin by Edmond J. Fitzgerald, 1964. Oil, framed, 40 x 32. Commissioned by the Naval War College.

Vice Admiral Charles L. Melson
July 31, 1964–January 25, 1966

Vice Admiral Charles L. Melson graduated from the Naval War College in 1948 and served on the staff the following year. During his presidency Melson supported greater emphasis on basic naval subjects, and he expanded the use of the Naval Electronic Warfare Simulator (NEWS) for the use of war-gaming in both the senior and junior courses. It was during his term also that an addition was made to Mahan Hall for an expanded library collection.

Painting of Vice Admiral Charles L. Melson by Edmond J. Fitzgerald. Oil, framed, 37 x 30. Commissioned by the Naval War College.

Vice Admiral John T. Hayward
February 15, 1966–August 30, 1968

A high school dropout and a bat boy for the New York Yankees, Vice Admiral John T. Hayward began his naval career in May 1925 as a recruit at the Newport Naval Training Station. Subsequently he would graduate from the Naval Academy Class of 1930, and enjoy a career marked by a driving desire for professional excellence through education. His Naval War College presidency was characterized by a dynamic program to make over the Navy's highest professional school along the lines of civilian colleges. The focus on professional curriculum, student requirements, and faculty was complemented also by a program for appropriate facilities that would ultimately lead to the construction of Spruance, Conolly, and Hewitt Halls during the 1970s.

Painting of Vice Admiral John T. Hayward by Edmond Fitzgerald, 1967. Oil, framed, 36 x 46. Commissioned by the Naval War College.

Vice Admiral Richard G. Colbert
August 30, 1968–August 17, 1971

Richard Gary Colbert (1915–1973) graduated from the Naval War College in 1956. Staying on at the Naval War College, he became the first director of the new senior foreign officers' course, eventually named the Naval Command College, that began in 1956 and had its first graduates in 1957. As the College's thirty-fifth President, he consolidated and strengthened the academic programs initiated by his predecessor, and he set in motion the construction program for Spruance, Conolly, and Hewitt Halls. Colbert also laid the groundwork for the Naval Staff College course for intermediate-level international officers, established the Naval War College Foundation, and instituted the biennial meeting of the world's chiefs of navy, the International Sea Power Symposia. From Newport, he went on to be Chief of Staff to the Supreme Allied Commander, Atlantic, and then, promoted to four-star rank, he became Commander in Chief, Allied Forces Southern Europe.

Painting of Vice Admiral Richard G. Colbert by Adrian Lamb, 1971. Oil, framed, 33 x 44. Loan from Navy Art Collection, Naval History and Heritage Command.

Vice Admiral Benedict J. Semmes, Jr.
August 17, 1971–June 30, 1972

Vice Admiral Benedict J. Semmes, Jr. came to the presidency of the College with thirteen years as a flag officer and many years in top level Navy Department Administration. He was no stranger to Newport, having served as a commander of the Cruiser-Destroyer Force, Atlantic, 1963–1964, and during that time he lectured on more than one occasion at the Naval War College. During his tour the College shifted its emphasis away from foreign and international affairs to management concepts in keeping with the prevailing notions of Washington.

Painting of Vice Admiral Benedict J. Semmes, Jr. by Tony Sarro, 1972. Oil, framed, 33 x 44. Commissioned by the Naval War College.

Vice Admiral Stansfield Turner
June 30, 1972–August 9, 1974

The presidency of Vice Admiral Stansfield Turner witnessed revolutionary changes that substantially changed the character of the College. Turner's most significant accomplishment was the establishment of a teaching methodology that demanded more individual effort from the students. This was achieved by the hiring of a permanent civilian faculty, instituting a long and required list, setting aside large amounts of time for individual student reading and writing, requiring term papers, making examinations mandatory, establishing highly structured seminars, and grading students on their performance. Turner left the College at the end of a two-year tour to become Commander of the Second Fleet. Subsequently he became Commander-in-Chief, Allied Forces, Southern Europe, and then Director of Central Intelligence in the administration of his Naval Academy classmate, President Jimmy Carter.

Painting of Vice Admiral Stansfield Turner by Jeanne Bunkley, 1974. Oil, framed, 39 x 31. Commissioned by the Naval War College.

Vice Admiral Julien J. Le Bourgeois
August 9, 1974–April 1, 1977

The focus of the administration of Vice Admiral Julien J. Le Bourgeois was the consolidation and refinement of the radical changes in curriculum made by the previous administration. Admiral Le Bourgeois also initiated action with the Navy Department leading to the creation of a Center for Advanced Research in 1980. Noteworthy, too, was a project initiated in 1976 for a museum of naval warfare and Navy regional history in the College's original home, Founders Hall. The building had been Naval Station headquarters until 1974, when it reverted to the College.

Painting of Vice Admiral Julien J. Le Bourgeois by Tony Sarro, 1976. Oil, framed, 36 x 30. Commissioned by the Naval War College.

Rear Admiral Huntington Hardisty
April 1–October 13, 1977

Huntington Hardisty (1929–2003) had been a captain and the Dean of Academics under Vice Admiral Julien J. Le Bourgeois, 1976–1977. As a newly promoted flag officer, he succeeded Le Bourgeois in April 1977 as the College's thirty-ninth President. His six-month tour as President is the shortest of all and characterized by a conscientious application to carrying on academic programs inaugurated by his predecessor. He later went on to serve as a four-star admiral as Vice Chief of Naval Operations, 1987–1988, and Commander in Chief, United States Pacific Command, 1988–1991.

Painting of Rear Admiral Huntington Hardisty by Tony Sarro. Oil, framed. Acquired through the Naval War College Foundation.

Vice Admiral James B. Stockdale
October 13, 1977–August 22, 1979

In 1965 Vice Admiral James B. Stockdale commanded Carrier Air Wing 16 and was shot down and taken prisoner by the North Vietnamese. Upon his release from captivity nearly eight years later, Stockdale was promoted to Rear Admiral and was awarded the Congressional Medal of Honor for the valor and heroism of his leadership while Senior Officer in prison camp. As College President, Stockdale expanded the elective program to include courses on a wide variety of topics, some of which relate indirectly or not at all to naval warfare and cognate themes.

Painting of Vice Admiral James B. Stockdale by Margaret Sargent, 1979. Oil, framed, 31 x 41. Acquired through the Naval War College Foundation.

Rear Admiral Edward F. Welch, Jr.
August 22, 1979–August 17, 1982

Edward F. Welch (1925–2008) was born in Barrington, Rhode Island. He was a graduate of the National War College and former dean of academic affairs at that institution. From 1977 to 1979, he was deputy director of international negotiations on the Joint Staff with responsibility to the Joint Chiefs of Staff for arms control talks. In addition, he played a key role on the U.S.-U.S.S.R. Standing Consultative Commission in 1977–1978. He was a member of the delegation that accompanied President Jimmy Carter to the SALT II summit in Vienna in June 1979. As the forty-first President of the Naval War College, he emphasized fleet operations in the curriculum and in war gaming. It was during his administration that global war gaming was begun. Welch also instituted a program, with the approval of the Chief of Naval Operations, for naval officer students to work for master's degrees with area colleges and universities.

Painting of Rear Admiral Edward F. Welch, Jr. by George Sottung, 1982. Oil, framed, 37 x 46. Acquired through the Naval War College Foundation.

Vice Admiral James E. Service
October 14, 1982–July 12, 1985

A naval aviator and test pilot, James E. Service had flown combat missions in both the Korean and Vietnam wars. A graduate of the Army War College, he had served as Commander, Battle Force, Sixth Fleet, and had been in that position when F-14 fighters from his battle force had shot down two Libyan aircraft during operations in the Gulf of Sidra. As the forty-second President of the Naval War College, Vice Admiral Service presided over the College's centenary in 1984, which was marked with the reopening of an enlarged museum in Founders Hall, after a two-year renovation program, and the publication of *Sailors and Scholars*, a history of the institution's first one hundred years. After leaving the College, he went on to be Commander, United States Naval Air Force, Pacific Fleet, from 1985 to 1987.

Painting of Vice Admiral James E. Service by Margaret Sargent. Oil, framed. Acquired through the Naval War College Foundation.

Rear Admiral Ronald F. Marryott
August 8, 1985–August 12, 1986

Ronald F. Marryott (1934–2005) was a Navy aviator who in the mid-1960s taught naval history and the history of U.S. foreign policy, American government and politics, and international relations at the Naval Academy. On operational assignments, he flew patrol and surveillance operations in P-2V and P-3 aircraft over both the Atlantic and the Pacific and went on to command Patrol Squadron 90 and the Naval Air Station, Moffett Field, and as a flag officer commanded the Iceland Defense Force. He served seven tours in the Pentagon, including as Director of the Strategic Plans and Policy Division (Op-60) and as Assistant Deputy Chief of Naval Operations for Plans and Policy. As the forty-third President of the Naval War College, he promoted the College's role in formulating strategic ideas and refining concepts. On leaving the Naval War College, he was appointed Superintendent of the Naval Academy from 1986 to 1988. After his retirement from active duty in 1990, he became president and chief executive officer of the George C. Marshall Foundation, and then, president and chief executive of the Naval Academy Alumni Association, 1996–2000.

Painting of Rear Admiral Ronald F. Marryott by Tony Sarro. Oil, framed. Acquired through the Naval War College Foundation.

Rear Admiral John A. Baldwin, Jr.
September 2, 1986–August 11, 1987

Coming to the Naval War College as its forty-fourth President Rear Admiral Baldwin initiated the process that eventually led to the accreditation of the College for the granting of master's degrees that would occur officially in 1991. He also established an Institute for Strategic Studies to facilitate the accreditation process and to serve as a device to secure and retain quality faculty, and he successfully effected the restoration of the College Library after a tragic fire, which did substantial damage in the area. After leaving the Naval War College, he served as Director of the Strategic Plans and Policy Division (J-5) on the Joint Staff, responsible to the Chairman of the Joint Chiefs of Staff for the strategic direction of the armed forces. Baldwin's last assignment was as President of the National Defense University.

Painting of Rear Admiral John A. Baldwin, Jr. by Margaret Sargent. Oil, framed. Acquired through the Naval War College Foundation.

Rear Admiral Ronald J. Kurth
August 11, 1987–July 17, 1990

Ronald J. Kurth taught Russian at the Naval Academy, earned a Master of Arts degree in Public Administration and a Ph.D. in Russian studies at Harvard University. He served as Naval Attaché at the U.S. Embassy in Moscow between 1975 and 1977, and as U.S. Defense Attaché in 1985–1987. He served as Director, Politico-Military Policy and Current Plans Division, in 1981–1983 and Director of Long Range Planning, in the Office of the Chief of Naval Operations, 1983–1984. As the forty-fifth President of the Naval War College, Rear Admiral Kurth testified before Congress concerning Professional Military Education and the application of the Goldwater-Nichols legislation, conceived the idea that led to the accreditation of the Naval War College to award a Master of Arts degree, and began the long-term effort to construct a new building. After leaving active duty, Kurth served as President of Murray State University in Kentucky, Dean of Academic Affairs at the Air War College, and President of St John's Northwestern Military Academy in Wisconsin.

Painting of Rear Admiral Ronald J. Kurth by Margaret Sargent, 1990. Oil, framed.
Gift of the Naval War College Foundation.

Rear Admiral Joseph C. Strasser
July 17, 1990–June 29, 1995

Rear Admiral Joseph C. Strasser occupied the presidency for five years, longer than any other President in the history of the College. His tour was highlighted by accreditation of the College by the New England Association of Schools and Colleges for the award of a master's degree in National Security and Strategic Studies. The Admiral also presided over the radical change in focus of the College curriculum after the fall of the Berlin Wall and the dissolution of the Warsaw Pact. Important too were his successful efforts at acquiring Congressional Authorization for the construction of a Strategic Maritime Research Center (McCarty Little Hall) and the inauguration of U.S. combined war games with the United Kingdom and Russia (RUKUS). He later served as Executive Director of the Naval War College Foundation for six years, 2000–2006.

Painting of Rear Admiral Joseph C. Strasser by Ted Tihansky. Oil, framed.
Acquired through the Naval War College Foundation.

Rear Admiral James R. Stark
June 29, 1995–July 24, 1998

The administration of Rear Admiral James R. Stark witnessed the reorganization of the curriculum of the College of Continuing Education so that officers could complete the course in a single shore tour. The administration also oversaw the design and building of McCarty Little Hall, initiated long-term planning for a new library and administration building and effected the incorporation of the Navy Warfare Development Command into College operations.

Painting of Rear Admiral James R. Stark by Margaret Sargent. Oil, framed. Acquired through the Naval War College Foundation.

Vice Admiral Arthur K. Cebrowski
July 24, 1998–August 22, 2001

The Navy's expert on network-centric warfare, Admiral Cebrowski became the 48th President of the Naval War College during a change of command ceremony at Colbert Plaza on July 24, 1998. When he became President, he was the first three-star admiral to lead the school since Vice Admiral James B. Stockdale in 1979. The role of the College was changing dramatically, in facilities, courses, and administration. In an address to an incoming class, Admiral Cebrowski called the War College the Navy's "intellectual center of gravity." After retirement from active duty, he was appointed Director of the Office of Force Transformation in the U.S. Department of Defense. He served in that position from 2001 until 2005.

Painting of Vice Admiral Arthur K. Cebrowski by Margaret Sargent. Oil, framed. Acquired through the Naval War College Foundation.

Rear Admiral Rodney P. Rempt
August 22, 2001–July 9, 2003

Taking command as President of the Naval War College only twenty days before the Terrorist Attack of 11 September 2001, Rear Admiral Rempt immediately refocused the College and its intellectual resources on the new imminent threats to the nation. Under his leadership, the College provided an illuminating series of point papers to the nation's top military and civilian leaders and initiated innovative homeland security games with participants from key local, state, and federal agencies. During his tenure, Admiral Rempt completed a wide-ranging review of the Navy's graduate and professional education policy that resulted in significant changes and improvements. Bringing widespread visibility to the works of the College, he increased student numbers in the College's resident, international, and distant education programs.

Painting of Rear Admiral Rodney P. Rempt by Tom Edgerton. Oil, framed. Acquired through the Naval War College Foundation.

Rear Admiral Ronald A. Route
July 9, 2003 August 12, 2004

Reporting to the Naval War College from duty as Commander, Navy Warfare Development Command, Rear Admiral Route accelerated the advantages that the Naval War College brought to the Navy and the nation by sharpening the College's focus on mission and relevance. Under his leadership, the College successfully addressed key operational challenges of significant concern to the Navy through an aggressive program of research, analysis, and war gaming. These efforts included establishing an advanced research program for selected students—the Halsey Scholars—collaborating with Navy experts in areas such as ballistic missile defense and theater antisubmarine warfare. Admiral Route also shaped the annual ethics conference to focus on the ethical and moral challenges that graduates would face as they returned to their services and re-entered the Global War on Terrorism. Hosting Vice Admiral Uriy Sysuev, Russian Federal Navy, Chief of the Kuznetsov Naval Academy in St. Petersburg, during a conference that facilitated frank discussions between retired Soviet Naval officers and their American couterparts, Rear Admiral Route set the stage for future opportunities for research, collaboration, and curriculum enrichment between the two premier war college institutions.

Painting of Rear Admiral Ronald A. Route by Tom Edgerton. Oil, framed.
Acquired through the Naval War College Foundation.

Rear Admiral Jacob L. Shuford
August 12, 2004–November 6, 2008

Rear Admiral Jacob Shuford, the fifty-first President of the Naval War College, led the College through an unprecedented period of mission growth, program expansion, and increased international engagement. He directed an extensive restructuring of the basic curriculum, and created and implemented the flag-level Joint Force Maritime Component Commander course, the Maritime Staff Operators Course, and a re-chartered Operational Planner Course. At the strategic level, under his direction, the College played the key role in designing the overall process for the nation's maritime strategy as well as planning and executing the geostrategic analysis that supported it. Admiral Shuford conducted personal diplomacy with his counterparts around the world to produce a network of naval colleges and associated institutions to work collaboratively on global maritime security issues. He established a series of regional symposia and reunions for the College's International Program graduates and a series of flag-level courses with partner navies in the different regions of the world. These efforts contributed to nearly doubling the number of navies participating in the International Seapower Symposium to ninety-eight, thus constituting the single largest gathering of naval leadership in history.

Painting of Rear Admiral Shuford by Margaret Sargent, 2007. Acquired through the Naval War College Foundation.

The Naval War College has a complete collection of oil portraits on canvas depicting every College President since 1939. Of the twenty-two Presidents of the Naval War College who served before 1939, there are only ten individuals who are not currently represented in this collection:

- Captain Charles Herbert Stockton
  President, 10 May 1893–2 November 1893
  and 2 November 1898–25 October 1900

- Rear Admiral French Ensor Chadwick
  President, 25 October 1900–16 November 1903

- Rear Admiral John Porter Merrell
  President, 24 May 1906–6 October 1909

- Rear Admiral Raymond Perry Rodgers
  President, 6 October 1909–20 November 1911

- Captain William Ledyard Rodgers
  President, 20 November 1911–15 December 1913

- Rear Admiral Austin Melville Knight
  President, 15 December 1913–16 February 1917

- Rear Admiral Clarence Stewart Williams
  President, 3 November 1922–5 September 1925

- Rear Admiral Harris Laning
  President, 16 June 1930–13 May 1933

- Rear Admiral Luke McNamee
  President, 3 June 1933–29 May 1934

- Rear Admiral Charles Philip Snyder
  President, 2 January 1937–27 May 1939

Above: Stephen B. Luce's grave, 2003. U.S. Navy Photo.

"War in certain circumstances may be averted. But mark this well. It may be averted in one way only, and that is to be fully prepared for it. That is the meaning of this college; it is an instrumentality for the prevention of war by being prepared for it."

STEPHEN B. LUCE, 1905

"The Naval War College forced me, for the very first time in my Navy career, to think globally and strategically. As a Navy Medical Department officer I tended to focus more on just patient care. The education I received from the Naval War College helped to mold me into a more rounded, better informed Naval officer capable of working in today's dynamic joint environment.

"I feel so strongly about the importance of the education and training received at the Naval War College as a part of an officer's professional development, I've made it a requirement for promotion to senior ranks within the Navy Medical Service Corps."

Rear Admiral Michael H. Mittelman, U.S. Navy
Director, Medical Service Corps

Missions and Traditions

Illustration by Tony Sarro.

NAVAL WAR COLLEGE MISSIONS AND STRATEGIC TRADITIONS

The Naval War College (NWC) holds fast to the belief, first articulated by its Founding President, Rear Admiral Stephen Bleecker Luce, USN, that *"The War College is a place of original research on all questions relating to war and to statesmanship connected with war, or the prevention of war."* Vice Admiral Stansfield Turner, USN, the College's thirty-seventh President, added focus and specificity to that depiction of the character of the institution when he charged the College to *"Always keep in mind the product which this country needs is military leaders with the capability of solving complex problems and executing their decisions. Scholarship for scholarship's sake is of no importance to us. You must keep your sights set on decision making or problem solving as your objective."*

The intents of Luce and Turner constitute the tradition, purpose, and strategic guidance of the Naval War College. Taken together, they are this institution's "anchor to windward." This tradition is more than rhetoric; it has a very practical and steadfast influence on everything that the College does. The four primary missions of the College are:

Developing Strategic and Operational Leaders Able to Serve Effectively in Peace and War. The College provides professional military education programs that are current, rigorous, relevant, and accessible to the maximum number of qualified U.S. officers and Navy enlisted personnel, civilian employees of the U.S. Government and non-governmental organizations, and international officers. The desired effect is to create a group of leaders of character who have trust and confidence in each other and are operationally and strategically minded, critical thinkers, proficient in joint matters, and skilled naval and joint warfighters.

Helping to Define the Future Navy and Its Roles and Missions. The College conducts research, analysis, and gaming to support the requirements of the Secretary of the Navy, the Chief of Naval Operations, the Combatant Commanders, the Navy Component Commanders, the Navy's numbered fleet commanders, other Navy and Marine Corps commanders, the U.S. Intelligence Community, and other departments and agencies of the U.S. Government. The desired effect is a program of focused, forward-thinking and timely research, analysis, and gaming that anticipates future operational and strategic challenges; develops and assesses strategic and operational concepts to overcome those challenges; assesses the risk associated with these concepts; and provides analytical products that inform the Navy's leadership and help shape key decisions.

Enhancing the Combat Readiness of the Nation's Maritime Forces. The College conducts training, education, leadership and assessment activities to support the ability of the Navy's Joint Force Maritime and Navy Component Commanders to function effectively as operational commanders. This effort shall include supporting the needs of the Combatant Commanders, Navy Component Commanders, and the Navy's numbered fleet commanders for operational planning, analysis, and war gaming to respond to emerging operational requirements. The desired effect is to improve the capability of Navy commanders to lead maritime, joint and combined forces and their staff members to plan, execute and assess and function cohesively as a maritime headquarters organization.

Strengthening Maritime Security Cooperation for a More Resilient Peace. The College brings together senior and intermediate level naval officers from other countries to develop leaders for high command in their navies; understand and evolve operational planning methods; create opportunities for expanded, high-level professional exchange through venues such as the International Seapower Symposium, Regional Symposia, formal college-to-college relationships with international counterparts, international publications, and alumni relations; and establish a regional studies structure to focus resources for greater impact in building and extending maritime partnerships. The desired effect is to build more robust and productive international maritime relationships, to improve the ability to operate effectively with partner nations, and to improve maritime security cooperation.

THE COLLEGE'S ORGANIZATION FOR EDUCATION

In recent years, the U.S. Naval War College accomplished a dramatic reshaping of the school's mission and curriculum, highlighting a pressing need for the Navy to develop leaders who can "support and lead as full partners in the joint operational arena." The Navy's move down the newly established Professional Military Education (PME) continuum, as one "that will systematically and comprehensively develop Navy flag officers experienced, schooled, and ready to lead maritime forces in the complex, joint multinational operations that characterize the new security environment." At the same time the War College began to lead an effort to develop a coherent Leadership Development Continuum focused on developing leaders of character who are prepared for operational and strategic leadership challenges.

The College is organized to provide education to groups of resident and nonresident students at various points in their careers. The major segments include:

The College of Naval Warfare (for U.S. students) and the ***Naval Command College*** (for senior international officers) are ten-month courses that seek to create graduates who are:

- Skilled in formulating and executing strategy and U.S. (or home nation) policy.

- Skilled in joint war-fighting, theater strategy, and campaign planning.

- Capable of strategically minded critical thinking.

- Capable of excelling in positions of strategic leadership.

These two Colleges educate 270 students per year with a student body composed of approximately 39% Navy students, 19% international, 14% from the U.S. Army, 9% from the U.S. Air Force, 8% from the U.S. Marine Corps, 8% from civilian government agencies, and 1% from the U.S. Coast Guard.

The ***College of Naval Command and Staff*** (for U.S. students) and the ***Naval Staff College*** (for intermediate-level international students) are ten-month courses that seek to create graduates who are:

- Skilled in applying Operational Art to maritime, joint, interagency and multi-national war-fighting.

- Skilled in Joint and Navy planning processes.

- Capable of critical thought with operational perspectives.

- Prepared for operational-level leadership challenges.

- Effective maritime spokespersons.

These two Colleges educate 325 students per year with a student body composed of approximately 56% Navy students, 12% international, 12% from the U.S. Army, 9% from the U.S. Air Force, 8% from the U.S. Marine Corps, 2% from civilian government agencies, and 1% from the U.S. Coast Guard.

The ***College of Distance Education*** develops and administers tailored versions of the College of Naval Command and Staff's Professional Military Education programs to nonresident military officers and selected government employees. The expected learning outcomes of these courses mirror those of the resident Command and Staff program. Courses are offered through a variety of means, including:

- The Fleet Seminar Program at 20 satellite campuses around the country that enrolls nearly 1,200 students annually.

- The Naval War College extension program at the Naval Postgraduate School in Monterey which offers 1,320 seats to NPS students annually.

- The Web-Enabled Command and Staff course which enrolls 1,100 students per year.

- The CD-ROM-based Command and Staff Course which enrolls another 1,100 students annually.

Additionally, the College of Distance Education offers primary, basic and introductory Professional Military Education courses on the Navy Knowledge Online system. Over 20,000 officers and enlisted personnel have enrolled in these courses since their inception over the last two years.

The ***College of Operational and Strategic Leadership:*** Throughout its history, the Naval War College has been involved in leadership development of those officers attending its courses. Recent developments expanded the Naval War College's role in educating future operational and strategic leaders. In response to these new responsibilities, the College of Operational and Strategic Leadership was formally established at the Naval War College on 1 October 2007 to direct and coordinate all efforts in the Leadership continuum of Professional Military Education (PME) for Navy officer and enlisted personnel including education on ethics and character development; operational level educational programs including Joint/Combined Force Maritime Component Commander (JFMCC/CFMCC) flag courses, Maritime Staff Operators Course (MSOC) and the Assist and Assess Team (AAT); Navy Senior Mentor program; Senior Enlisted Academy (SEA) and the Stockdale Group advanced research program in operational level leadership. The College has also established a Professional Military Ethics Program that provides a series of lectures, panels, seminars and discussion groups to further officers' understanding and application of ethical leadership.

COSL is comprised of three directorates:

- The Research and Analysis/Competency Development Directorate, which is responsible for Mission Essential Competencies (MEC) and Maritime Operations Centers (MOC) Manpower Training & Education Requirements.

- The Operational Level Programs (OLP) Directorate, which is responsible for Joint Flag Officer Education (JFMCC/CFMCC) courses, the Assist and Assess Team (AAT), Maritime Staff Operators Course (MSOC) to include Battle Lab, and Senior Mentors.

  • The Joint Force Maritime Component Commander Flag Course is the senior Navy PME course. Its purpose is to prepare 1- and 2-star U.S. flag officers to serve as maritime operational commanders.

  • The Combined Force Maritime Component Commander Flag Course is offered to both U.S. and international Flag Officers. It is regionally focused and normally hosted at navy component headquarter locations.

  • C/JFMCC Flag Courses educate 60–70 flag officers annually.

  • The AAT supports Geographic Combatant Commander certification of Joint Force Maritime Component Commanders and assesses fleet maritime headquarters/MOCs to support U.S. Fleet Forces Command in accrediting these MOCs.

  • MSOC is a five-week course that educates about 700 students each year and, while supporting broader efforts to build expertise at the operational level of war, enhances the Navy's ability to prepare personnel to effectively serve in operational-level maritime staffs with solid familiarization and guided practical experience.

  • The Navy's Senior Mentor program supports Naval War College flag-level professional military education and provides on-site support to the U.S. Navy's fleet commanders and their staffs. Senior mentors are also used in senior advisory positions at other forums where the Navy requires a presence. The Navy's Senior Mentor program consists of retired admirals with extensive joint and navy experience.

- The Leadership Directorate, which is responsible for Leadership Elective courses, Professional Military Ethics, James Bond Stockdale Group, and the Senior Enlisted Academy.

THE COLLEGE'S ORGANIZATION FOR RESEARCH

The ***Center for Naval Warfare Studies.*** The Center for Naval Warfare Studies serves as a nexus for broadly based, advanced research on the naval contribution to a national strategy. The Center directly complements the curriculum at the Naval War College by providing a place for researching important professional issues which, in turn, inform and stimulate the faculty and students in the classroom.

Additionally, the Center links the Naval War College to the fleet and policymakers in Washington by serving as a focal point, stimulus, and major source of strategic and campaign thought, by integrating strategic, campaign, and tactical concepts, by linking strategic concerns with technological developments, and finally, by testing and evaluating concepts through war gaming. The research staff is organized into six departments:

Strategic Research Department: Produces studies, research reports, and briefings formulated in accordance with traditional research methods and standards. Some projects are internally generated, while others are written in response to requests from Navy and Marine Corps officials, including the Chief of Naval Operations, or from operational commanders including unified commanders.

Warfare Analysis and Research Department: The Warfare Analysis and Research Department conducts research into current and future war-fighting issues using select NWC students working under the mentorship of experienced research professionals. The collaborative research is coordinated through one of the Halsey or the Mahan Scholars research groups while individual research work is guided by faculty in CNWS and throughout the College as appropriate. Under the management of the Warfare Analysis and Research Department, the Decision Support Center (DSC) provides an innovative environment specifically designed to bring together a range of tools to aid in decision-making, concept development or alternative analysis and is available for use by the College, DoD, the Department of the Navy and other government agencies.

War Gaming Department: Conducts approximately 50 games yearly in support of internal College needs and externally generated requests from various branches of the Defense and Navy departments, operational commands and civilian agencies, including the Office of the Vice President of the United States, the Joint Chiefs of Staff, and the Secretary of the Navy. The War Gaming Department employs a wide variety of gaming techniques ranging from complex, multi-sided, computer-assisted games to simpler, single-sided seminar games, and game foci can range from broad national strategies to the specifics of tactics.

International Law Department: Provides analytical support to the Department of the Navy and the Department of Defense on rules of law and broad oceans law and policy issues arising in the interagency arena, often responding to specific tasking generated by the Chief of Naval Operations, the Commandant of the Marine Corps, the Judge Advocate General, and fleet commanders.

Maritime History Department: Serves as the central resource and contact point for the entire Naval War College in matters relating to maritime history. The Department specializes in the history of the theory and practice of naval and maritime strategy, the history of naval operations in all periods, the history of naval activities in the Narragansett Bay region since the age of exploration, and the history of the Naval War College since 1884.

Naval War College Press: Publishes, on a quarterly basis, the *Naval War College Review*, which focuses on politico-military, strategic, and operational matters. The NWC Press also publishes the Newport Papers and full-length books.

MISSIONS AND TRADITIONS

NWC Provost, Ambassador Mary Ann Peters, introduces guest speaker in Pringle Auditorium.

Defense Secretary Robert Gates addresses students and faculty on his vision for the Defense Department in 2010 and beyond. Navy Photo by MCC Robert Inverso.

HEROES

"Our heroes are those who act above and beyond the call of duty and in doing so give definition to patriotism and elevate all of us. America is the land of the free because we are the home of the brave."

David Mahoney

Snowstorm, 2003. U.S. Navy Photo.

On any given day, one can walk the old halls of the College in search of the inspiration and passion for knowledge that inspired the likes of Luce and Mahan. Around every corner, treasures of our country's past are found. Who were these men with portraits on the wall and buildings named after them? Were there more discoveries to be made that could be added to such a rich and prestigious heritage?

With recently gained knowledge of the Naval Battle of Guadalcanal, the pages of history became more understandable and Admiral Frank Jack Fletcher's career proved to be the template for answering an important question: How many Naval War College graduates earned our country's highest honor?

The answer: 15. Lieutenant Commander W. A. Edwards was the aide to Admiral Sims, Rear Admiral Isaac C. Kidd served on the staff, Captain A. H. Rooks served on the strategy senior class staff and Vice Admiral J. B. Stockdale served as President. Captain W. R. Rush was the first graduate to earn the Medal of Honor having graduated from the Naval War College in 1905. Vice Admiral H. P. Huse and Rear Admiral E. A. Anderson were the first Medal of Honor recipients to attend the Naval War College in 1916. A total of ten students attended courses at the Naval War College after having been recognized for their gallantry in combat.

Although research depicts only U.S. Navy and Marine Corps personnel, more treasures are left of our alumni's past unwritten for the next student searching for inspiration and original thought. The century-old saying has not lost its point, that "the winds and waves are always on the side of the ablest navigators." These men proved their worthiness as scholars and on the fields of battle. More importantly, this institution either prepares us for great opportunities or it rewards us with a great opportunity.

Iwo Jima Memorial by Felix de Weldon, 2003. U.S. Navy Photo.

Admiral Frank F. Fletcher, USN
(1855–1928)
NWC Class of 1917
Medal of Honor, 1914

Captain William R. Rush, USN
(1857–1940)
NWC Class of 1905
Medal of Honor, 1914

Vice Admiral Harry McL. P. Huse, USN
(1858–1942)
NWC Class of 1915
Medal of Honor, 1914

Rear Admiral Edwin A. Anderson, USN
(1860–1933)
NWC Class of December 1916
Medal of Honor, 1914

Major General William P. Upshur, USMC
(1881–1943)
NWC Class of 1932
Medal of Honor, 1915

Rear Admiral Isaac C. Kidd, USN
(1884–1941)
NWC Staff 1937–1939
Medal of Honor, 1941

Captain Willis Winter Bradley, USN
(1884–1954)
NWC Class of 1938
Medal of Honor, 1917

Admiral Frank Jack Fletcher, USN
(1885–1973)
NWC Class of 1932
Medal of Honor, 1914

Lt. Cmdr. Walter A. Edwards, USN
(1886–1928)
NWC Aide to the President, 1919–1921
Medal of Honor, 1922

Heroes

Captain Mervyn Sharp Bennion, USN
(1887–1941)
NWC Class of 1935
Medal of Honor, 1941

Captain Franklin Van Valkenburgh, USN
(1888–1941)
NWC Class of 1934
Medal of Honor, 1941

Rear Admiral Norman Scott, USN
(1889–1942)
NWC Class of 1935
Medal of Honor, 1942

Admiral Oscar C. Badger II, USN
(1890–1958)
NWC Class of 1939
Medal of Honor, 1914

Captain Albert H. Rooks, USN
(1891–1942)
NWC Staff 1939–1941
Medal of Honor, 1942

Rear Admiral Samuel G. Fuqua, USN
(1899–1987)
NWC Class of 1944
Medal of Honor, 1941

Rear Admiral Richard Nott Antrim, USN
(1907–1969)
NWC Class of 1947
Medal of Honor, 1942

Rear Admiral Richard H. O'Kane, USN
(1911–1994)
NWC Class of 1956
Medal of Honor, 1944

Vice Admiral James Bond Stockdale, USN
(1923–2005)
NWC President, 1977–1979
Medal of Honor, 1976

NWC Graduation, 2002. U.S. Navy Photo.

IMAGES OF THE COLLEGE

Images by Bernie Dunn.

THE CAMPUS
DEWEY FIELD

Admiral of the Navy George Dewey (1837–1914)

Dewey Field is named in honor of Admiral of the Navy George Dewey, the only officer of the U.S. Navy to ever hold the rank. He was born on 26 December 1837, in Montpelier, Vermont. On 23 September 1854, he was appointed Acting Midshipman from the First Congressional District of Vermont, and upon graduation from the U.S. Naval Academy in June 1858, was warranted Midshipman. He is best known as the Victor of Manila Bay during the Spanish-American War, of 1898. Dewey Field is also the U.S. Navy's first drill field.

Above: Admiral Dewey. U.S. Navy Historical Archives.

THE CAMPUS

Dewey Field flagpole, 2004. U.S. Navy Photo.

Dewey Field on a foggy morning, 2004. U.S. Navy Photo.

THE CAMPUS

Inset: Dewey Field, circa 1930s. Naval War College Museum.

47

NWC flagpole cannons, 2003. U.S. Navy Photo.

Flagpole Cannons

The flagpole cannons are from the captured Spanish cruiser *Reina Mercedes*. USS *Reina Mercedes* was a cruiser captured by the U.S. Navy during the Spanish-American War. She was named in honor of Queen Mercedes of Spain when she was built at Cartagena in 1887. She served under Admiral Cervera in the defense of Santiago, Cuba, although her boilers and engines were in very poor shape and much of her armament had been removed to be used for shore batteries.

Raised after the war, she was towed to Newport, Rhode Island in 1904, where she served as a receiving ship. After a refit in 1912, she was transferred to Annapolis, Maryland to serve as a station ship, replacing USS *Hartford*.

Above: *Reina Mercedes.* **Photo prior to 1898, U.S. Naval Historical Center #NH-61231.**

"The in-depth study of Department of Defense bureaucracy, military operations and strategy provided a broad theoretical background for what I would be doing [in the future]. The joint nature of the school and the opportunity for independent study served to significantly broaden my exposure to areas outside my limited Air Force flying operations background. It was a challenging year but remarkably rewarding."

General Bruce Carlson, U.S. Air Force
Commander
Air Force Materiel Command

Above: Gen Bruce Carlson, 2007. Air Force Photo.
Right: Founders Hall, 2003. U.S. Navy Photo.

THE CAMPUS

International Park

USS *Constellation* anchor, 2008. Photo by JD DuVall.

USS *Constellation* Anchor

This anchor from the USS *Constellation*, which now is docked in Baltimore, Maryland, is located in International Park, commemorating the naval heritage of Narragansett Bay—a heritage which extends from the foundation of the nation in the American Revolution. The *Constellation* served as a receiving and training ship at the Newport Naval Training Station from 1894 to 1946.

The anchor was removed from the ship in 1906 and has been on display since then at various sites on Coasters Harbor Island. It is reputed to have been manufactured during the first half of the nineteenth century and is one of the oldest of its kind. It weighs 6000 lbs. and measures 13 feet (shank) by 15 feet 8 inches (stock). Each fluke is 45 inches long by 42 inches wide.

Beside the pathway is a memorial plaque to the late Esau Kempenaar, a Dutch immigrant who worked as a gardener for residents of mansions in nearby Newport and later became a successful businessman. Mr. Kempenaar was a strong supporter of NWC International Programs for many years.

The USS *Constitution* served as a training ship of the Naval Apprentice System in the 1870s, when the system was commanded by Capt. Stephen B. Luce. The ship and others came to Newport in 1880 and then in 1884 when the Naval War College opened. The USS *Constitution* is now berthed in Boston.

Inset: *Old and New Ironsides.* **Painting by Francis West, Naval War College Museum.**

Quarters AA

The official residence of the President of the Naval War College and his family is a three-story, wood frame, colonial revival building situated on the southeast corner of the college campus on Coasters Harbor Island, Newport. It was constructed in 1896 at a cost of $16,226 as the residence of the Commandant of the Naval Station, a command which then (1894–1898) incorporated the Naval Training Station, the Naval Torpedo Station on Goat Island, and the Naval War College. The first President to occupy the building, in 1903, was Captain French E. Chadwick, who was also Commandant of the Second Naval District. Until 1913 it was occupied at intervals by college Presidents and commanders of the Naval Station. Thereafter, it was used exclusively by college Presidents.

Officially designated Quarters AA on the naval reservation, but more popularly known as the President's House, it was added to the National Register of Historic Places in 1989. The building underwent several significant structural changes over the years. Shortly after its completion in 1896, a conservatory ("Palm Room") was added on to the east living room and the library. In 1909 a two-story annex, incorporating bathrooms on the second and third floors and a service stairway, was built on the back. Three years later the conservatory was extended northward, the length of the east side, and made into a large reception room open to both the east living room and the dining room. The front of the conservatory, meanwhile, was extended outward to encompass an area that had been a semicircular open porch. Finally, in 1939, a new and somewhat larger porch (present sun parlor) replaced the west porch, and the entrance from the west living room was widened. Today, the building contains 8,770 square feet of space on three floors, divided into twenty-five rooms, including nine bedrooms and six baths.

The President's House is the scene of frequent visits by distinguished persons from all walks of life and from all parts of the world. Receptions and other social affairs associated with college operations are held here. Public areas of the quarters are decorated by both the U.S. Navy and the Naval War College Foundation. In this latter case, individuals, among whom are earlier occupants of the quarters, have donated articles through the Foundation, which seeks to preserve the historic ambiance of the quarters.

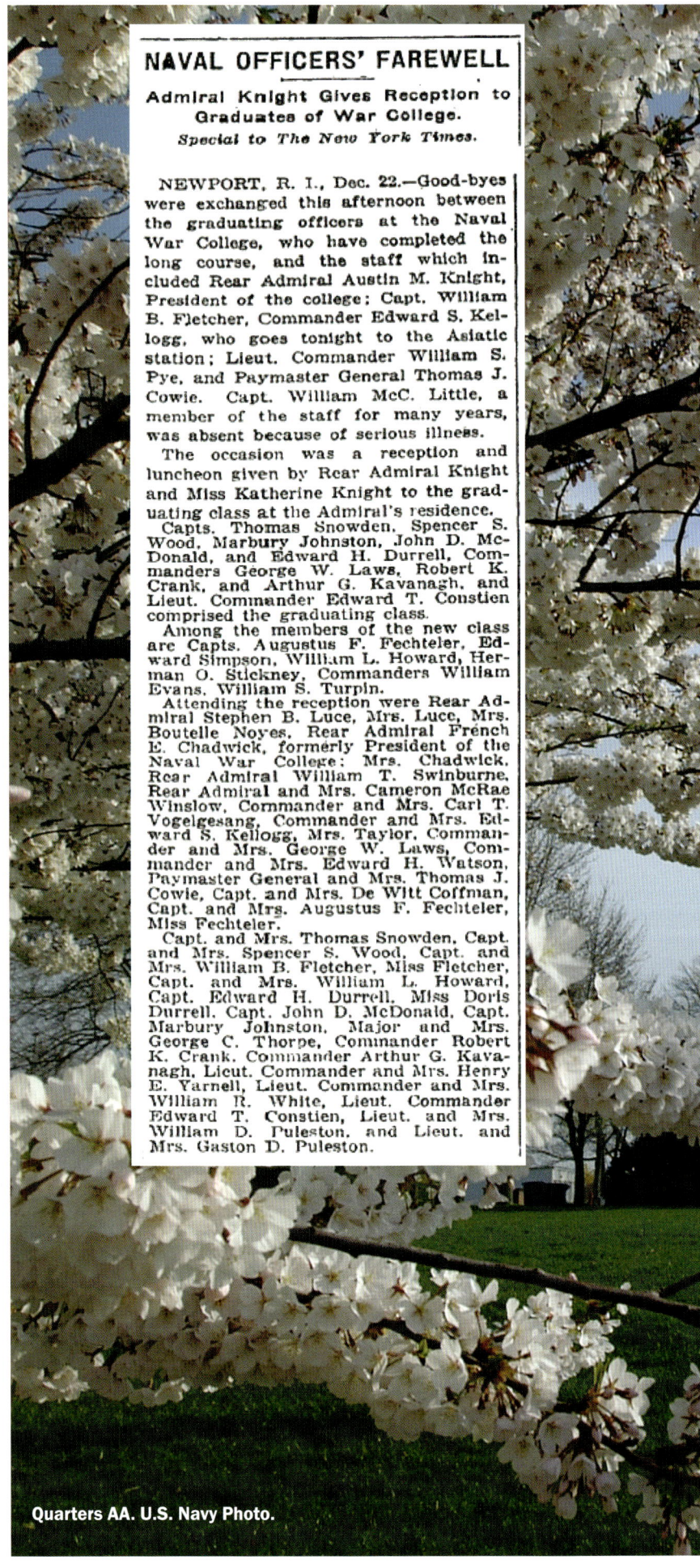

Quarters AA. U.S. Navy Photo.

NAVAL OFFICERS' FAREWELL

Admiral Knight Gives Reception to Graduates of War College.

Special to The New York Times.

NEWPORT, R. I., Dec. 22.—Good-byes were exchanged this afternoon between the graduating officers at the Naval War College, who have completed the long course, and the staff which included Rear Admiral Austin M. Knight, President of the college; Capt. William B. Fletcher, Commander Edward S. Kellogg, who goes tonight to the Asiatic station; Lieut. Commander William S. Pye, and Paymaster General Thomas J. Cowie. Capt. William McC. Little, a member of the staff for many years, was absent because of serious illness.

The occasion was a reception and luncheon given by Rear Admiral Knight and Miss Katherine Knight to the graduating class at the Admiral's residence.

Capts. Thomas Snowden, Spencer S. Wood, Marbury Johnston, John D. McDonald, and Edward H. Durrell, Commanders George W. Laws, Robert K. Crank, and Arthur G. Kavanagh, and Lieut. Commander Edward T. Constien comprised the graduating class.

Among the members of the new class are Capts. Augustus F. Fechteler, Edward Simpson, William L. Howard, Herman O. Stickney, Commanders William Evans, William S. Turpin.

Attending the reception were Rear Admiral Stephen B. Luce, Mrs. Luce, Mrs. Boutelle Noyes, Rear Admiral French E. Chadwick, formerly President of the Naval War College; Mrs. Chadwick, Rear Admiral William T. Swinburne, Rear Admiral and Mrs. Cameron McRae Winslow, Commander and Mrs. Carl T. Vogelgesang, Commander and Mrs. Edward S. Kellogg, Mrs. Taylor, Commander and Mrs. George W. Laws, Commander and Mrs. Edward H. Watson, Paymaster General and Mrs. Thomas J. Cowie, Capt. and Mrs. De Witt Coffman, Capt. and Mrs. Augustus F. Fechteler, Miss Fechteler.

Capt. and Mrs. Thomas Snowden, Capt. and Mrs. Spencer S. Wood, Capt. and Mrs. William B. Fletcher, Miss Fletcher, Capt. and Mrs. William L. Howard, Capt. Edward H. Durrell, Miss Doris Durrell, Capt. John D. McDonald, Capt. Marbury Johnston, Major and Mrs. George C. Thorpe, Commander Robert K. Crank, Commander Arthur G. Kavanagh, Lieut. Commander and Mrs. Henry E. Yarnell, Lieut. Commander and Mrs. William R. White, Lieut. Commander Edward T. Constien, Lieut. and Mrs. William D. Puleston, and Lieut. and Mrs. Gaston D. Puleston.

"I have really enjoyed my time at NWC and know that it is a superb and very 'joint' institution that enables military and civilians to grow and learn in a historic setting at a great facility. Graduates from all services have told me throughout the past 10 years that their time at NWC enabled them to finally 'get it' about the need for joint education and the importance of all services in joint and coalition warfare."

Vice Admiral John G. Cotton, U.S. Navy
Former Chief of Navy Reserve

Above: VADM John G. Cotton, 2007. U.S. Navy Photo.
Left: Pakistan CNO Lunch at President's House, 2007. U.S. Navy Photo.

Photo of Luce Hall, 1972.
Inset: Order from Commo Stephen B. Luce, 1885. U.S. Naval Historical Center.

Luce Hall

Luce Hall was the first purpose-built building for the Naval War College. Built in 1892, it was named after the first President of the Naval War College, Rear Admiral Stephen B. Luce. It is now a National Historical Landmark. It was designed by George Champlin Mason, who was inspired by the Antwerp Guild Halls, Belgium. The stones came from Fall River, Massachusetts. It was the main building of the College until 1974 and now houses the Naval Command College (the senior international officers' course) and the College of Distance Education (the College for non-resident students wanting to take classes centered around the teachings of the resident courses).

Admiral Luce was instrumental in developing the first curriculum of the College. He introduced lectures, readings and seminars as a way to make the transition from a month-long course to an intensive one year professional naval study. He equipped the faculty with the tools to recruit not only naval officers, but those from other services and civilian sectors, which is still the hallmark of the War College curriculum and faculty programs today. Wanting to give faculty and students the means to become better professional military officers, he founded the NWC's study of strategy, tactics and operations based on a core of history. The man he chose to develop the College's initial naval history course was Captain Alfred Thayer Mahan, who became a vital contributor to the development of the Naval War College's prestige and curriculum.

Top: Admiral Luce's portrait. Photo by Mr. Joe Quinn, 2007.
Bottom: Photo of Naval War College, 1935. Naval War College Museum.

Pringle Hall

This building was named after Rear Admiral Joel R. P. Pringle, President of the Naval War College from 1927 to 1930, who was instrumental in its construction. Pringle Hall was opened in 1934 to house the College's auditorium and to serve as the war gaming maneuver room. War gaming continued here until 1957 when the first computer-generated gaming facility was established in Sims Hall. The war gaming that was done in the late 1930s for War Plan Orange in preparation for WWII was done in Pringle Hall.

The artist Graham Sutherland (1903–1980) was commissioned by Parliament to paint Churchill's portrait to mark his 80th birthday in 1954. On its unveiling, Churchill, who was himself an amateur artist, acidly remarked: "The portrait is certainly a remarkable example of modern art. It combines force with candor. . . ." Although Churchill was only to have the loan of the portrait during his lifetime, Lady Churchill destroyed the original painting by 1956.

Above: Admiral Joel R. P. Pringle's portrait. Photo by Joe Quinn.

Above: John Mackay's copy of Graham Sutherland's portrait of Winston Churchill, 2008. Photo by JD DuVall.
Opposite: Pringle Hall, 2004. U.S. Navy Photo.

Fascinated by the story, Murray Davis commissioned the British artist John Mackay (1937–) to paint this replica of the Sutherland portrait in 1988.

For many years, Mackay's copy of the Sutherland portrait hung at Café Zelda on Thames Street, Newport. In June 2003, Murray Davis and Constance Metcalf donated the portrait to the Naval War College Foundation for display in Pringle Hall.

MAHAN HALL

Built in 1904, Mahan Hall was named in 1936 after the great educator and naval strategist—and a former President of the Naval War College—Rear Admiral Alfred Thayer Mahan. Mahan Hall houses the Rotunda, library stacks and the conference center, which is still in use today to host conferences and events. The display cases in the Rotunda hold gifts to the College from former international students. Mahan was one of the four original faculty members. He wrote and delivered speeches about maritime power, the role of fleets in expanding sea power, and the contribution of seapower on the greatness of a nation. In 1890, he published *The Influence of Seapower Upon History, 1660–1783*. This book made him one of the best known U.S. naval officers of the day and made the Naval War College an internationally respected institution. Mahan's views would influence great leaders such as Theodore Roosevelt and Henry Cabot Lodge, who would help shape America's future at the turn of the century.

Left: Mahan Rotunda, 2003. U.S. Navy Photo.

Hall of Flags

The flags between Mahan and Luce Halls contain the national colors of the international students in residence at the Naval Command College. The flags between Mahan and Pringle Halls contain the national colors of the international students in residence at the Naval Staff College.

Three portraits are hung under a beautiful 1900-era stained-glass ceiling: Admiral Kalbfus on the right, Admiral Richmond K. Turner, the famous amphibious commander in the Pacific War and pre-WWII Naval War College faculty member, center, and Admiral Caspar Goodrich, a protégé of Admiral Luce, left.

Spanish cannons from the Spanish-American War were melted down and cast to form the light posts on the handrails and the column "caps" in the Mahan Rotunda. They were made specially for the Naval War College at the Washington Gun Factory, now the Washington Navy Yard.

Above: *Reina Mercedes,* **1898. DoD Media #HD-SN-99-01947.**

Mahan stairwell, 2003. U.S. Navy Photo.

Felix de Weldon Passageway

Since Wars Begin in the Minds of Men,
It Is in the Minds of Men
That Defenses of Peace
Must Be Constructed
Preamble to the UNESCO Constitution

The passageway connecting the older buildings of the College and the new academic complex contains sculptured bas reliefs depicting our nation's conflicts from the Revolutionary War to Vietnam and mankind's "conquest of the moon" by Dr. Felix de Weldon, a life-long benefactor and friend of the College. Dr. de Weldon is perhaps best known for his famous Iwo Jima Memorial in Arlington, Virginia.

Felix de Weldon used the words from the United Nations Educational, Scientific and Cultural Organization (UNESCO) preamble during his dedication address of the passageway in the 1970s.

Felix de Weldon's contribution to the College has been a never-ending fountain of inspiration for students understanding warfare.

Above: Felix de Weldon Passageway, 2003. U.S. Navy Photo.

AMERICAN REVOLUTION—BATTLE OF YORK TOWN

THE SPIRIT OF '76

WAR OF 1812

CONFEDERACY

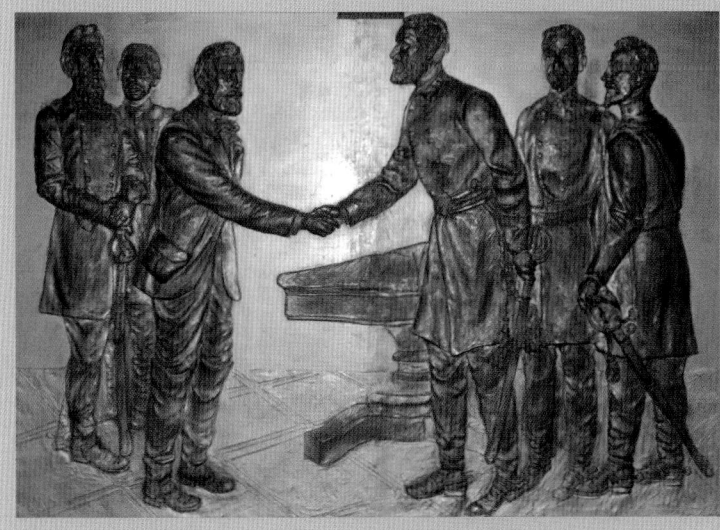

CIVIL WAR—APPOMATTOX

UNION

Sculptured reliefs by Felix de Weldon, photographed by JD DuVall, 2008.

Sculptured reliefs by Felix de Weldon, photographed by JD DuVall, 2008.

CONQUEST OF THE MOON

Sculptured relief by Felix de Weldon, photographed by JD DuVall, 2008.

Spruance Hall

Spruance Hall was the first structure built in a major building program in the 1970s. Named after Admiral Raymond A. Spruance, a World War II hero, and former President of the College, this building was opened 7 December 1972. The auditorium seats up to 1100 people and is host to numerous lectures and conferences.

Admiral Spruance served four tours of duty at the College and molded the Naval War College curriculum into two specific areas of study: strategy and tactics, and strategy and logistics, which would be built around war gaming. He also wanted to educate officers in the greater problems of national affairs. As a WWII veteran, he gave lectures on a wide variety of subjects and focused *The Naval War College Review* and introduced the Current Strategy Forum, all which still exist today.

The auditorium was extensively renovated in 2009, and was rededicated in time to host the 19th International Sea Power Symposium in October 2009.

Above: Admiral Stansfield Turner's NWC Address, April 2004, Spruance Auditorium. U.S. Navy Photo.

THE CAMPUS

General David Petraeus, U.S. Central Command, addresses students in the newly renovated Spruance Auditorium. U.S. Navy Photo.

Naval Staff College reception, 2008. U.S. Navy Photo.

"The Junior course at Naval War College was the first time in my career that I worked, studied and socialized with officers from all the other branches of our Navy and other armed services. I came to value not only my fellow Navy Surface Warfare Officer, Submarine, Medical, Chaplin and Supply officers but also officers from the Army, Air Force and Marine Corps. Their culture, way of approaching an issue, and values were all unique and I could learn from all of them. I find that later in my Navy career I still have contacts across service lines and can reflect on the differences I saw then that make our military great.

"Lastly, the College allowed me the time to think as an adult—I learned to write outside our military style, to comprehend military and political philosophy, and to value education as something that made me a better officer and, dare I say, fighter pilot."

Vice Admiral Thomas J. Kilcline, U.S. Navy
Commander, Naval Air Forces

Above: VADM Thomas J. Kilcline, 2007. U.S. Navy Photo.

Conolly Hall

A second new academic building was opened in 1974. Named after a former President of the College, Admiral Richard L. Conolly, the building houses the staff and faculty of the College, administrative offices, and medical and dental offices.

On the 2nd floor, known as the President's Passageway, are the offices of the President, Provost, and other senior leaders, and the Turner Conference Room. On the 3rd and 4th floors are faculty offices and seminar rooms.

Throughout the building students view a gallery of over twenty Naval War College presidential portraits as well as oil paintings and prints of numerous naval engagements from American history.

Left: Conolly Hall. U.S. Navy Photo.

Turner Conference Room

The presidency of Vice Admiral Stansfield Turner witnessed revolutionary changes that substantially changed the character of the College. Turner's most significant accomplishment was the establishment of a teaching methodology that demanded more individual effort from the students. This was achieved by the hiring of a permanent civilian faculty, instituting a long and required reading list, setting aside large amounts of time for individual student reading and writing, requiring term papers, making examinations mandatory, establishing highly structured seminars, and grading students on their performance.

Turner left the College at the end of a two-year tour to become Commander of the Second Fleet. Subsequently he became Commander-in-Chief, Allied Forces, Southern Europe, and then Director of Central Intelligence in the administration of President Jimmy Carter.

Right: Turner Dedication, April 29, 2004. U.S. Navy Photo (painting of Vice Admiral Stansfield Turner by Jeanne Bunkley).

Student Seminar on Colbert Plaza, 2003. U.S. Navy Photo.

"The year spent at the Naval War College was both personally and professionally rewarding, and opened an aperture on the other services not previously enjoyed. While I must confess to not having been as studious as I might have been, I do very vividly recall the intensely interesting dialogue among professionals that [was] a daily fixture and which helped shape my professional development at a critical juncture in my career."

General William S. Wallace, U.S. Army
Former Commander, United States Army Training and Doctrine Command

Above: General William S. Wallace, 2007. U.S. Army Photo.

Hewitt Hall. U.S. Navy Photo.

Hewitt Hall

Hewitt Hall opened in 1976. It is named after Admiral H. Kent Hewitt, a graduate and former faculty member of the College. It houses the Eccles Library, the cafe, classrooms, and the College of Distance Education faculty offices and administrative spaces. College of Naval Warfare class photos are located on the second deck, covering the classes of 1983 to 2004. College of Naval Command and Staff class photos are located on the third deck, covering the same period.

Admiral H. Kent Hewitt was born in Hackensack, New Jersey, on 11 February 1887 and graduated from the U.S. Naval Academy in 1906. Prior to his promotion to flag rank, Admiral Hewitt served aboard several battleships and destroyers, including USS *Missouri* (BB 11), USS *Connecticut* (BB 18), USS *Flusser* (DD 20), USS *Florida* (BB 30), and USS *Pennsylvania* (BB 38). He commanded USS *Eagle*, USS *Cummings* (DD 44), USS *Ludlow* (DD 112), Destroyer Division 12 and USS *Indianapolis* (CA 35). During the 1920s and 1930s, he was involved in naval gunnery and ordnance as Pacific Fleet Gunnery Officer and Inspector of Ordnance in charge of the Naval Ammunition Depot at Puget Sound, Washington, while sharpening his knowledge of shore bombardment so necessary in his later amphibious assaults.

In April 1942, Admiral Hewitt took command of the amphibious forces in the Atlantic Fleet. He distinguished himself during landings in North Africa in late 1942. In July 1943, Admiral Hewitt's Eighth Fleet conducted the first Allied amphibious landings of Europe in World War II. It was this amphibious assault on Sicily that landed General George Patton and his Third Armored Division that ultimately led to the surrender of Fascist Italy. Admiral Hewitt retired in 1949 and passed away in 1972 in Orwell, Vermont.

Above: Admiral H. Kent Hewitt's portrait. Photo by JD DuVall, 2008.

Henry E. Eccles Library

"*An educational institution is a combination of people and ideas. The Naval War College is an institution of selected men and women whose common purpose is to generate and develop ideas associated with maritime power and naval warfare, in all their aspects. Therefore, I take special satisfaction that in having this library named for me, I become associated with great men such as Luce, Mahan, Sims, Pringle, Spruance, Conolly and Hewitt. Each of these in his special way was a great man in the naval profession. Each generated and developed ideas relative to sea and maritime powers, naval warfare and naval education. They set high standards of personal integrity and dedication to which we all can aspire. The library is the heart and focus of this vision of greatness and this generation and development of ideas.*"

From Admiral Eccles' remarks at the dedication of the library on 10 June 1985.

Above: Photo by JD DuVall of the painting of Rear Admiral Henry E. Eccles by Tony Sarro.

On 10 June 1985, the College library was named in honor of Rear Admiral Henry E. Eccles, a noted logistician, strategist, and author whose association with the College spanned thirty-eight years. The library is central to Naval War College educational and research programs. Admiral Eccles and his ship, USS *John D. Edwards,* participated in the battle of Badung Strait, and shortly after, while assigned to the American-British-Dutch-Australian Command, the battle of the Java Sea. Wounded in action, he was later awarded the Navy Cross, the Silver Star, and The Netherlands Order of the Bronze Lion.

Located in Hewitt Hall, the library houses over 245,000 books, journals, documents, and over 540,000 microforms. The academic collection emphasizes subjects and disciplines of interest to the profession of arms, naval and military science, history and strategy, international relations, management, economics, international law, and contemporary world issues.

A classified collection within the main library contains an additional sixty-five thousand print and twenty thousand microform documents, classified (up to SECRET) and unclassified, dealing with defense systems, area studies, naval warfare publications, and Naval War College papers and lectures. The library's rare book collection features a number of unique works on naval and military science.

Above: Students in Eccles Library, 2004. U.S. Navy Photo.

McCarty Little Hall

The Strategic Maritime Research Center (SMRC) officially opened in September 1999. It is named after Captain William McCarty Little, an influential leader and the leading innovator in the early development of naval war gaming. This state-of-the-art facility is used for conducting war games, decision support, research and analysis, and conferences. The building is designed to accommodate the kinds of technology necessary for supporting multimedia presentations, video teleconferencing, and computer networking systems that are essential for war gaming. This three-story building contains approximately 103,000 square feet and houses approximately 250 staff and students. The first floor contains a 160-seat, stadium-style auditorium as well as a large gaming floor. The second floor includes four large and eight small game cells used for operational play, as well as the Decision Support Center. The third floor is highlighted by the Joint Command Center, patterned on various operational command centers used for joint task force commanders. In addition, this floor has a high-tech conference room and six academic classrooms.

McCarty Little Hall also houses offices for the Center for Naval Warfare Studies, including the Decision Strategies Department, the Strategic Research Department, and International Law Department. Additionally, the Office of Naval Intelligence Detachment and the Meteorology and Oceanography Detachment are located here.

Left: McCarty Little Hall, 2003. U.S. Navy Photo.
Above: Decision Support Center, 2003. U.S. Navy Photo.

"The mission of the Naval War College is to develop operational and strategic leaders. Attending the NWC Junior Course was the primer that elevated me out of my comfort zone of tactical employment and gave me the groundwork to think critically at the operational and strategic levels of war. The development of critical thinking, combined with the school's emphasis on joint and interagency operations, is the key to success for today's military leader.

"The experiences of NWC provided me the impetus of strategic vision that the US military services are joint, co-equal, interdependent partners that cohesively support national security objectives. Furthermore, the foundation I gained proved invaluable in preparing me for my role on the Joint Staff, the Air Staff, and even for my current role as Commander, Air Combat Command."

General John D. W. Corley, U.S. Air Force
Former Commander, Air Combat Command

Above: General John Corley, 2007. Air Force Photo.
Left: Partnership with China Conference, 2007. U.S. Navy Photo.

Patriots Memorial

Monument was made from shattered Indiana limestone recovered from the West Facade of the Pentagon.

Above: Naval War College's Patriots Memorial, 9-11-03. U.S. Navy Photo.

THE CAMPUS

*In Memory of
Naval War College
Students and Alumni
Who Gave Their Lives
While Serving the Nation*

CAPT GERALD F. DECONTO, USN
LCDR ROBERT R. ELSETH, USNR
CAPT LAWRENCE D. GETZFRED, USN
Ms. ANGELA M. HOUTZ, DON
LCDR PATRICK J. MURPHY, USNR
LT JONAS M. PANIK, USNR
CAPT JACK D. PUNCHES, JR., USN (Ret.)
CDR ROBERT A. SCHLEGEL, USN
CDR DAN F. SHANOWER, USN
MAJ KIP P. TAYLOR, USA

**The Pentagon, Washington, D.C.
September 11, 2001**

Above: 9/11 Memorial Dedication Ceremony visitors honor the fallen as the American flag is flown at half-mast in front of McCarty Little Hall, September 11, 2003. U.S. Navy Photo.

Sims Hall, 2004. U.S. Navy Photo.

Sims Hall

Sims Hall was built as Naval Training Station Barracks C in 1904. It was acquired by the Naval War College in 1946, when it was named Sims Hall. Sims Hall is named for one of our early and greatest instructors and leaders, Admiral William S. Sims, also a former President of the College. While President of the College, Admiral Sims directed the curriculum to concentrate more heavily on the practical and immediate aspects of naval education. He established the courses of command, strategy, tactics and policy, versions of which are still in use today. Sims Hall was used until 1999 as the College's war gaming facility.

Today, it houses the Navy Warfare Development Command (NWDC). NWDC was founded at Newport, RI, in July 1998 by the Chief of Naval Operations, Admiral Jay Johnson, as a part of the reorganized Naval War College. He personally chartered the NWDC to focus and champion warfare innovation and concept development, to identify the capabilities which must flow from concepts, to design, plan and coordinate the Navy's Fleet Battle Experiment program, to synchronize, approve and disseminate Navy doctrine, and to represent the Navy in joint experimentation.

NWDC is moving to Norfolk, Virginia in FY-10 as part of the Base Realignment and Closure (BRAC) process.

Inset: Admiral Sims. Image from Charles Carlisle Taylor, *The Life of Admiral Mahan* (London, 1920), Pg. 170.

Schonland Hall

Schonland Hall was named after Rear Admiral Herbert E. Schonland, who received the Medal of Honor for his actions in the Naval Battle of Guadalcanal. The decision to name the building that once housed the Damage Control Assistant (DCA) school after Rear Admiral Herbert Emery Schonland was an obvious and deliberate one.

During World War II, while serving in the cruiser *San Francisco* (CA 38) as DCA, then Lt. Cdr. Schonland led the successful struggle to save the heavily battle-damaged ship with great professionalism and a display of personal courage that won for him the Medal of Honor. Rear Admiral Schonland was the only DCA officer in WWII to be so honored and his performance of duty stands as a continuing inspiration for all DCAs. In 2007, the building became a part of the Naval War College campus to meet the College's requirements for additional office space.

Above: Schonland Hall, 2007. U.S. Navy Photo.

Medal of Honor Citation:

"For extreme heroism and courage above and beyond the call of duty as damage control officer of the U.S.S. *San Francisco* in action against greatly superior enemy forces in the battle off Savo Island, 12–13 November 1942. In the same violent night engagement in which all of his superior officers were killed or wounded, Lt. Cmdr. Schonland was fighting valiantly to free the *San Francisco* of large quantities of water flooding the second deck compartments through numerous shell holes caused by enemy fire. Upon being informed that he was commanding officer, he ascertained that the conning of the ship was being efficiently handled, then directed the officer who had taken over that task to continue while he himself resumed the vitally important work of maintaining the stability of the ship. In water waist deep, he carried on his efforts in darkness illuminated only by hand lanterns until water in flooded compartments had been drained or pumped off and watertight integrity had again been restored to the *San Francisco*. His great personal valor and gallant devotion to duty at great peril to his own life were instrumental in bringing his ship back to port under her own power, saved to fight again in the service of her country."

Ernest E. Evans Hall

Ernest Edwin Evans, born 13 August 1908 in Pawnee, Oklahoma, graduated from the Naval Academy in 1931. During World War II, he commanded *Alden* (DD-211), and later *Johnston* (DD-557). Commanding *Johnston* he was awarded the Bronze Star for meritorious achievement in action against a Japanese submarine on 16 May 1944, and in the Battle of Leyte Gulf fought his ship gallantly until it was sunk, 25 October 1944, by the Japanese force superior in number, firepower, and armor. Commander Evans was posthumously awarded the Medal of Honor for his material contribution to the decisive victory won in Leyte Gulf and shared in the Presidential Unit Citation awarded his group for this action in which he gave his life.

Above: Evans Hall. Photo by JD DuVall, 2008.
Bottom: Cmdr Evans. U.S. Naval Historical Center photograph.

INTERNATIONAL PLAZA

The International Plaza was dedicated on 13 July 1976 to the graduates of the Naval Command College who have served the cause of peace with distinction by their contribution to international friendship and cooperation. The plaza is located between Pringle Hall and Spruance Hall on the harbor side of the College's campus.

Top: Colbert Plaza Flags, 2003. U.S. Navy Photo.

Bottom: Intl. Plaza, 2008. U.S. Navy Photo.

Above: This Victorian vision in marble of Columbus discovering America was given to the Naval War College by Edward J. Berwind (USNA, 1886), the coal magnate whose Newport summer cottage was "The Elms."

"The education I received at the Naval War College was far more than textbooks and lectures. The interaction with faculty and fellow students provided me the strategic foundation I would later need as the Chief of Media for US Central Command in the beginning of Operation Iraqi Freedom, and then later as the spokesman for the Chairman of the Joint Chiefs of Staff. My year at NWC was invaluable."

Rear Admiral Frank Thorp, U.S. Navy
Former Chief of Information

Bottom: RADM Frank Thorp, 2007. U.S. Navy Photo.

REFLECTIONS

"Without a doubt, one of the most significant influences in my professional life was the time I spent as a student at the Naval Command & Staff course in Newport. This wasn't training, this was education about our profession and about the broader security issues facing our nation. We were challenged to think broadly, to dig deeper, to challenge accepted practices and to produce better alternatives."

General John M. Shalikashvili, U.S. Army
Former Chairman, Joint Chiefs of Staff
(1993–1997)

Inset: General John Shalikashvili, 1997. U.S. Army Photo.

Reflections

Sunset view of the Newport Bridge, 2004. U.S. Navy Photo.

"The Naval War College senior course gave me the intellectual foundation I needed to be an effective O5 and O6. I know NWC helped make me a flag officer. In my two sea duty tours leaving Newport, I used what I learned in Strategy and Policy and Joint Military Operations to create and use—in combat—innovative concepts which were based on sound, historical doctrine and [principles].

"Focusing on the 'operational center of gravity' I was able to provide the Navy component Commander suitable and relevant targets for TLAM [Tomahawk land attack missile] tasking in Operation Allied Force against Kosovo. No senior officer should pass up a chance for the incredible opportunity of an education at the Naval War College."

Rear Admiral Tony L. Cothron, U.S. Navy
Former Director of Intelligence

"One of my NCC classmates is a Rear Admiral in the Indian Navy. At the end of the day every relationship comes down to individuals not to nations. If you can make that initial contact on the basis of someone that you mutually know then the initial engagement is warmer than it normally would be."

Rear Admiral David Ian Ledson
Former Chief of Navy
Royal New Zealand Navy

"I majored in Naval Architecture at Annapolis and then received a Masters in Civil Engineering at the University of Colorado. Until attending the Naval War College I had nothing approaching a 'liberal' education, but was focused almost exclusively on technical subjects. So I found the experience at Newport exhilarating. For the first time I focused deeply on the human side of events where the columns don't always add up and decisions are made amid uncertain[t]y.

"The War College staff created an environment within which we were encouraged to challenge the conventional wisdom and reject pat answers. We were made to assemble our own viewpoints, never frivolously, but by reasoning and logic, and then defend the answer. I can see clearly now, after 15 years, how I was being trained to COMMUNICATE, not a strong suit among all engineers, but an essential ingredient of good leadership."

Rear Admiral Greg Shear, CEC, U.S. Navy
Commander, Naval Facilities Engineering Command
Chief of Civil Engineers

"My time at the NWC brought me to the conclusion that I needed to learn how to think—and the time of reflection provided by my year in Newport helped me to gain much needed contextual thinking as I resumed my operational and staff postings. In fact, I can honestly say it provided me with most of the ingredients necessary for first rate thinking about strategy and operations with a rich variety of ideas to draw on."

Rear Admiral James P. Wisecup, U.S. Navy
Current President, Naval War College

"I recall my years at Navy Command and Staff College fondly. The course was academically demanding. The professors challenged us to leave our familiar world of tactics and operations to consider the broader import of national security. The wonderful academic and social environment also fostered new friendships and great respect across our services."

Lieutenant General Glenn F. Spears,
U.S. Air Force
Commander, 12th Air Force

Inset: Lieutenant General Glenn Spears, 2007. U.S. Air Force Photo.

Sunset view of Luce Hall, 2003. U.S. Navy Photo.

REFLECTIONS

BOAT DRILL, U. S. NAVAL TRAINING STATION. NEWPORT, R. I.

NAVAL TRAINING STATION FROM WATERFRONT, NEWPORT, R. I.

U. S. Naval War College

"I still consider the year I spent in Newport to be the premier educational experience of my career. The quality of the civilian faculty was probably the most striking characteristic that differentiated the Naval War College from the other professional military education experiences I have had. The faculty was populated with many brilliant academicians who were truly interested in expanding the 'military minds' of the student body.

"The difference between training and education is more than semantics. I have used the educational thought processes I encountered at the Naval War College to my personal advantage in every assignment I have had, including command in combat, over the past two decades. The college's focus on teaching students to write and speak clearly, to conduct convincing fact-based analysis, and to translate historical perspectives into modern problem solving in a highly critical academic setting is exactly what our nation's officer corps needs to succeed. Warfighting is serious business and the Naval War College impressed me because they took my education as seriously as I did at the time—and still do."

LtGen George J. Trautman III, U.S. Marine Corps
Deputy Commandant for Aviation

Above: Lieutenant General George Trautman III, 2007. U.S. Marine Corps Photo.

Naval Staff College Wardroom, 2004. U.S. Navy Photo.

NAVAL WAR COLLEGE ILLUSTRATED HISTORY AND GUIDE

Jim Thorpe competition 2007. U.S. Navy Photo.

Reflections

"As a young navy officer I was trained, not necessarily on purpose, to believe what I did as a submarine officer was the most important activity in the navy, possibly in the entire military. Upon arriving at the Naval War College it did not take long for me to realize what I did was important, but nowhere near as important as what my fellow service members did as disparate but interconnected joint arms of the U.S. Military. This enlightenment early in my career helped pave the way for me to always approach business from a joint perspective, this approach ultimately served me well in every senior level job to which I was assigned.

"On many occasions, since my days at the Naval War College, I have had the great pleasure of rekindling friendships with classmates from each service and civilians as well. The bonds forged from this experience made it easy to break the natural barriers that exist between the services and foster cooperative efforts. I was fortunate to have received the Naval War College education and experience and would recommend it to all officers."

Rear Admiral Bruce E. Grooms, U.S. Navy
Vice Director, Joint Staff

Above: Rear Admiral Bruce Grooms, 2009. U.S. Navy Photo.

Luce Hall cupola, 2004. U.S. Navy Photo

REFLECTIONS

"I cannot overstate the importance of what you are doing up in Newport. Your mission is a critical one. . . . I will tell you this: our nation has always—and will always—need adaptive, creative, and agile strategic leaders who can excel in ambiguity. Creating those leaders is the task to which you must continue to dedicate yourselves."

General Raymond T. Odierno, U.S. Army
Commanding General, Multi-National Force–Iraq

Above: General Raymond T. Odierno, 2009. U.S. Army Photo.

Above: U.S. Naval Training Station postcard from the personal collection of Professor John Jackson.

STATION. NEWPORT, R. I.

"I view my experience at the War College as one of the highlights of my career as a military chaplain. The Command and Staff course did in fact fulfill the promise of the Chief of Chaplains: it trained me in both the language and the issues of the line community, and empowered me to fulfill my role as moral/ethical advisor on a tactical, operational, and eventually strategic level. In fact, the program so sensitized me to the jus ad bellum/jus in bello issues of war that I eventually finished a doctorate in philosophy; my dissertation addressed some of the contemporary issues of just war, and in specific, the moral issues facing combatants in modern war.

"A decade later I was invited to guest lecture in military ethics at the Joint Forces Staff College (Hofheimer Lecturer 2005) and the Naval War College (Ethics Conference). The NWC also afforded me the opportunity to build friendships and begin networking with the military's future leaders, leaders from all the military services. These relationships remained fruitful, productive and invaluable throughout the rest of my career."

Louis V. Iasiello, OFM, RADM, CHC, U.S. Navy (Ret.)

Above: Lou Iasiello, 2008. Washington Theological Union Photo.

"The opportunity to serve as a Mahan Scholar at the U.S. Naval War College afforded me the time, resources, and flexibility to pursue a better understanding of national security issues across a very broad front—and then apply that understanding to a series of billets that increasingly drew on the knowledge I gained in Newport."

Rear Admiral Charles W. Martoglio, U.S. Navy
Director of Operations
U.S. Pacific Command

"NWC provided me by far the best educational experience that I have had during my career. The classes were relevant, the seminar format encouraged rich discussion and open exchange of ideas and the bonds with classmates have lasted these many years. I often refer back to my year in Newport as my sabbatical where I was given the opportunity to think, research and learn, the extent of which I have not experienced since.

"As I mentor junior officers I always encourage them to select NWC as their intermediate or senior service school."

Vice Admiral Nancy E. Brown, U.S. Navy
Former Director of Command, Control Communications, and Computer Systems J-6, The Joint Staff

"The Strategy & Policy as well as National Security Decision Making courses provided me some most useful insights into the manner in which the US system worked. In the later stages of my career, as I assumed positions of increasing responsibility, I found that I could apply a lot of what I had learnt in the NCC to situations arising at home.

"One of the most valuable gains from the year spent in Newport was the many friends one made world-wide. Thereafter, no matter which part of the world I visited I could count upon meeting either a NCC classmate, or a NWC graduate and striking a common chord. In my class, three of us made it to Chief: the Pakistani, the Japanese (who is currently the JCS) and myself. The Pakistani officer and I had become good friends because we were regular squash partners in Newport. The contacts that one made in the NWC were lifelong and most beneficial.

"There can be no doubt that military education has a vital role to play in shaping the senior leadership of the armed forces. However, it is important that such education should be as broad-based as possible, and focuses adequately on the humanities. It should serve to expand an individual's outlook and open the windows of his mind so that he can become a balanced senior officer."

Admiral Arun Prakash (Retired)
Former 18th Chief of Naval Staff
Indian Navy

"While assigned to the Wargaming Department, and the CNO's Strategic Studies Group, at the U.S. Naval War College during the early 1990s, I was exposed to many lessons, but one important lesson has formed the foundation of all I do as a naval officer and intelligence professional:

"Preparation. At the Naval War College, lessons regarding preparation were, literally, written on the gaming floors of Sims Hall. From the halcyon days of the inter-war era, the Navy's future leaders prepared for World War II by 'gaming' War Plan Orange and the other Rainbow plans. In the immediate post–Cold War era, the Strategic Studies Group prepared for an uncertain future by assessing alternative future scenarios.

"To conduct an exemplary wargame required weeks of detailed preparation. Depending upon the type of 'game' such preparation can include a behind-the-scenes development of scenarios, research and inclusion of historical anecdotes, and engagement with thought-leaders from across the military, academia, industry and society. This preparation adds to the richness of the game, and more-often-than-not, results in learning experiences of great magnitude for the game's participants.

"The great Spanish novelist and playwright, Miguel De Cervantes, wrote 'To be prepared is half the victory.' The U.S. Naval War College has consistently provided its students the education and opportunities that prepare the next generation of naval leaders for a future that is unknown and uncertain. This lesson of 'preparation' was embedded in my genes while at NWC and remains a fundamental element of how I look at the naval profession."

Vice Admiral David J. Dorsett, U.S. Navy
Deputy Chief of Naval Operations
for Information Dominance

Admiral's Barge on the Bay, 2003. U.S. Navy Photo.

"The battlefield will continue to be chaotic; continue to be uncertain; continue to have a lot of fog and friction. So we need individuals who can operate in that type of battlefield. And, that only comes, in my opinion, through education."

General Michael W. Hagee, USMC (Ret.)
33rd Commandant of the Marine Corps

Inset: General Michael Hagee, 2006. U.S. Marine Corps Photo.

"The Naval War College opened up my aperture by exposing me to national security challenges much more than a tactical single-service solution. We were challenged to think deeper and broader. Thinking through a strategy for addressing a national security issue stretched the limits of my experience and forced me to think at a level relatively unexplored at that point in my service. Campaign-level planning is a complex undertaking and the War College faculty were masterful in elevating my thought processes to address the strategic issues. You walk away from this experience with sharpened 'how-to-think' skills. The experience helped me expose gaps in my professional knowledge as well as develop skills in critical thinking. Without doubt, the War College education armed me with the tools to contribute in meaningful ways at the strategic and operational levels.

"The experience also gave me an appreciation for interdependencies and how we could best leverage the unique, but complementary capabilities each Service provides to a Joint commander. I think we gained an appreciation for each other's Service and realized how important relationships are across Service lines when we face tough strategic challenges. Terms such as 'unified action' took on much more meaning for me—we learned to understand the depth of coordination required to achieve a unified response to a challenge. In our educational experience, we reaffirmed that trust across Service lines was as fundamental to our success as guns, aircraft, and ships, perhaps more so. Even though our strategic challenges took place in the safety of the War College classroom, the lessons transferred to the realities we faced around the globe.

"At graduation, I felt much more prepared for the professional challenges that lay ahead. The Naval War College is an institution clearly focused on preparing leaders to operate at the highest levels of our government."

Lieutenant General Kevin T. Campbell, U.S. Army
Commander, U.S. Army Space and Missile Defense Command

REFLECTIONS

Admiral Mike Mullen, chairman of the Joint Chiefs of Staff, addresses students and faculty at the Naval War College 2010. U.S. Navy Photo.

"Getting naval personnel in uniform, people who are charged with the conduct and management of violence from diverse backgrounds, different ethnic backgrounds, social religious differences under one roof and making them come together for a period of one year is something which is unmatched anywhere else on this globe. It just goes on to prove that people when they are put together can integrate and talk and can come up with solutions that are to the benefit of mankind. The bonds and relationships which we all built during our one year stay over here are in fact to my mind investments in the long run. It is indeed a marvelous experience to know that someone else in another part of the world will respond to your requirement in case the need arises."

Vice Admiral Jagjit Singh Bedi, Indian Navy
Former Flag Officer Commanding-in-Chief of the Southern Naval Command

Inset: Vice Admiral Bedi, 2006. Indian Navy Photo.

Tall Ships, 2004. U.S. Navy Photo.

NWC Seal, 2008. Photo by JD DuVall.

"A 'HOME RUN!!!' is how I would describe my educational experience with the Naval War College. It was unlike any other professional military course that I had ever taken. Indeed, it was the highlight at that point in my career that benefited me greatly as I assumed General Officer responsibilities several years later. The framework for learning encouraged me to view National Security issues in a lens that included the whole of government of which the military was just one part. The lecture, small group discussion and subsequent large group Q & A was an attractive format to obtain an understanding of the issues, lay out the decisions made by the leaders, analyze the consequences of those decisions and discuss what we would have done as leaders. More importantly, the topics for the course were thought provoking, complex national security issues that were greatly enhanced by the delivery of each subject by top notch faculty and staff.

"As a General Officer, I have had a variety of commands and served on high level operational and service staffs where broad thinking on issues was critical to mission success. The time I spent at the Naval War College was instrumental in providing a strong foundation for my decision making responsibilities at these higher levels. I would not trade that experience for the world."

Major General Cornell A. Wilson, Jr.
U.S. Marine Corps
Commander, U.S. Marine Corps Forces South

"I attended the Naval War College as an in-residence intermediate service school student in the College of Naval Command and Staff. The first thing I found unique about this program was that the faculty and curriculum were the same for the ISS students as for the senior service school attendees. This meant that the focus of our ISS program was geared toward a more experienced officer and hence one who had a deeper appreciation and understanding of the role the military plays in support of our national strategic objectives. I was challenged to raise my sights and quality of my cognitive thought to another level . . . two pay grades. This program was the most challenging but rewarding education . . . civilian or military . . . I have been fortunate enough to attend throughout my entire professional life. Further, being an AF officer in a joint environment best prepared me for the command and senior joint warfighting positions that I have held.

"On a personal level, the NWC environment provided me and my family outstanding opportunities. We made friends that we continue to be close to today. Newport was a great place to tour visiting family and friends. Our son took a Tiger Cruise with the cub scouts. Two of our daughters played in a state championship soccer game and one caught her first fly ball while playing on a girls softball team. Barb and I have been back to stay in the visiting DV quarters and take in the view of the Narragansett Bridge. The whole experience has truly been one of the highpoints of my career."

Brigadier General Michael J. Basla, U.S. Air Force
Vice Commander, Air Force Space Command

"NWC was without a doubt the most enlightening experience in my Naval career. The outstanding curriculum highlights the importance of understanding military history, service capabilities, politics, media, and the critical role of joint Military Operations in executing National Strategy mandates. And, the curriculum is enhanced with the visits of respective Combatant Commanders who openly share valuable information on their area of operations.

"I personally encourage every Junior Officer to apply for NWC and highlight that the NWC experience provides an overarching DoD and Joint Service framework that will abet their future leadership roles."

Rear Admiral Michael C. Bachmann, U.S. Navy
Commander
Space and Naval Warfare Systems Command

"I graduated through the College of Continuing Education via distant learning, and was able to connect my work at the War College with my PhD work in international relations at Tufts University. The confluence of the two programs truly prepared me well for later jobs ranging from a Strike Group Commander to my current duties as Supreme Allied Commander of NATO."

Admiral James G. Stavridis, U.S. Navy
Commander, U.S. European Command,
Supreme Allied Commander, Europe

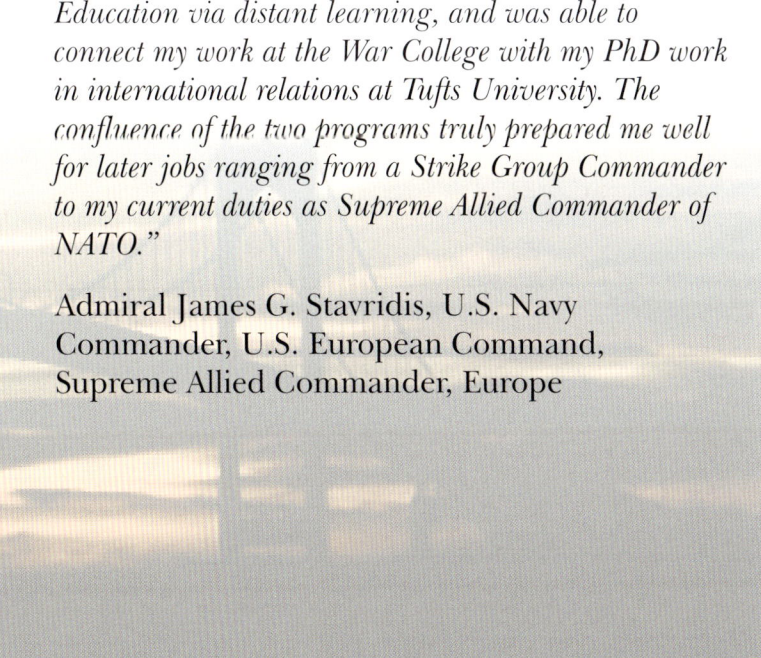

President's Cup Run, 2006. Official U.S. Navy Photo.

REFLECTIONS

"I had a great professional and personal experience at the NWC. It was both professional development and family time. The most important aspects of my education at the Naval Command and Staff College were the development of the ability to think through a complex issue, to put issues in context, and to quickly and succinctly identify core issues and potential courses of action. In my view, the Strategy and Policy portion of the curriculum was the cornerstone of this educational process. It provided an appreciation for the study of history and the military art, as well as the skills needed to get straight to the point in both writings and discussions."

LtGen George J. Flynn, USMC
Deputy Commandant for Combat Development and Integration

Above: LtGen George Flynn, 2007. U.S. Marine Corps Photo.

"Naval War College was a profound, thought provoking experience. I have benefitted not only from the superlative educational opportunity, but from the enduring relationships made at Newport that have served me well over the past 21 years."

Rear Admiral Allen G. Myers, IV, U.S. Navy
Director, Warfare Integration
OPNAV Staff N8F

"I attended NWC in the fall 1991 session. This was special for two reasons; first, it was a tremendous joint educational opportunity that was a real eye opener for a guy who had been 'Navy blue' his entire career. Second, this was the first 'Post Desert Storm' War College class, and many students from all services were coming fresh from combat. This gave the class a sense of relevance that was palpable. In the years since, even though my opportunities to serve in joint assignments have been limited, I look back on my time at the Naval War College as perhaps the most broadening 10 months of my 35 year Navy career. The opportunity to read, learn, interact and meet the challenge to think critically was truly special. To this day I remain thankful to my placement officer who rolled me from command early, over my objections, to study in Newport when what I really wanted to do was get in some post relaxation and play golf. It was a real life changer."

Vice Admiral Harold D. Starling, II, U.S. Navy
Commander, Naval Network Warfare Command

"Working with officers of the other services and nations was extremely beneficial. My joint tour at the European Command was enhanced by the interactions during my time at Newport. Theater Security Cooperation was a large part of my responsibilities and the one-year opportunity to learn about synergy with our friends, partners and allies was invaluable. Additionally, leadership of a Carrier Strike Group virtually requires this level of military education which is drawn upon on a daily basis when deployed."

Rear Admiral John W. Goodwin, U.S. Navy
Assistant Chief on Naval Operations
Next Generation Enterprise Network (NGen)

"My year at the College of Naval Command and Staff was an eye opening experience. Prior to arriving at Newport I had had the opportunity to fly in Operation Southern Watch and I worked with the Navy on several missions. Additionally, I instructed at the USAF Fighter Weapons School and controlled many Navy adversary air syllabus sorties. After working side by side in operational missions with Naval aviators, it was great to learn more about the joint fight from the College of Naval Command and Staff's perspective."

Brigadier General Lori J. Robinson,
Deputy Director for Force Application
and Support, Joint Staff

View of Naval War College, 1930s. NWC Museum.

"Naval War College was an awesome experience! The curriculum was expertly designed with a big to small framework: from a global perspective to specific battles that provided lessons learned. The historical examples provided invaluable context for leaders to view the world today and into the future. I left NWC with an enlightened view of the world and much better prepared to help our great nation defend liberty in the years to come. NWC is one of the few academic experiences I would like to repeat!"

Brigadier General Francis M. "Frank" Bruno, U.S. Air Force
Former Director of Logistics
Headquarters Air Force Materiel Command

Above: Brigadier General Francis Bruno, 2007. U.S. Air Force Photo.

Alumni of Distinction

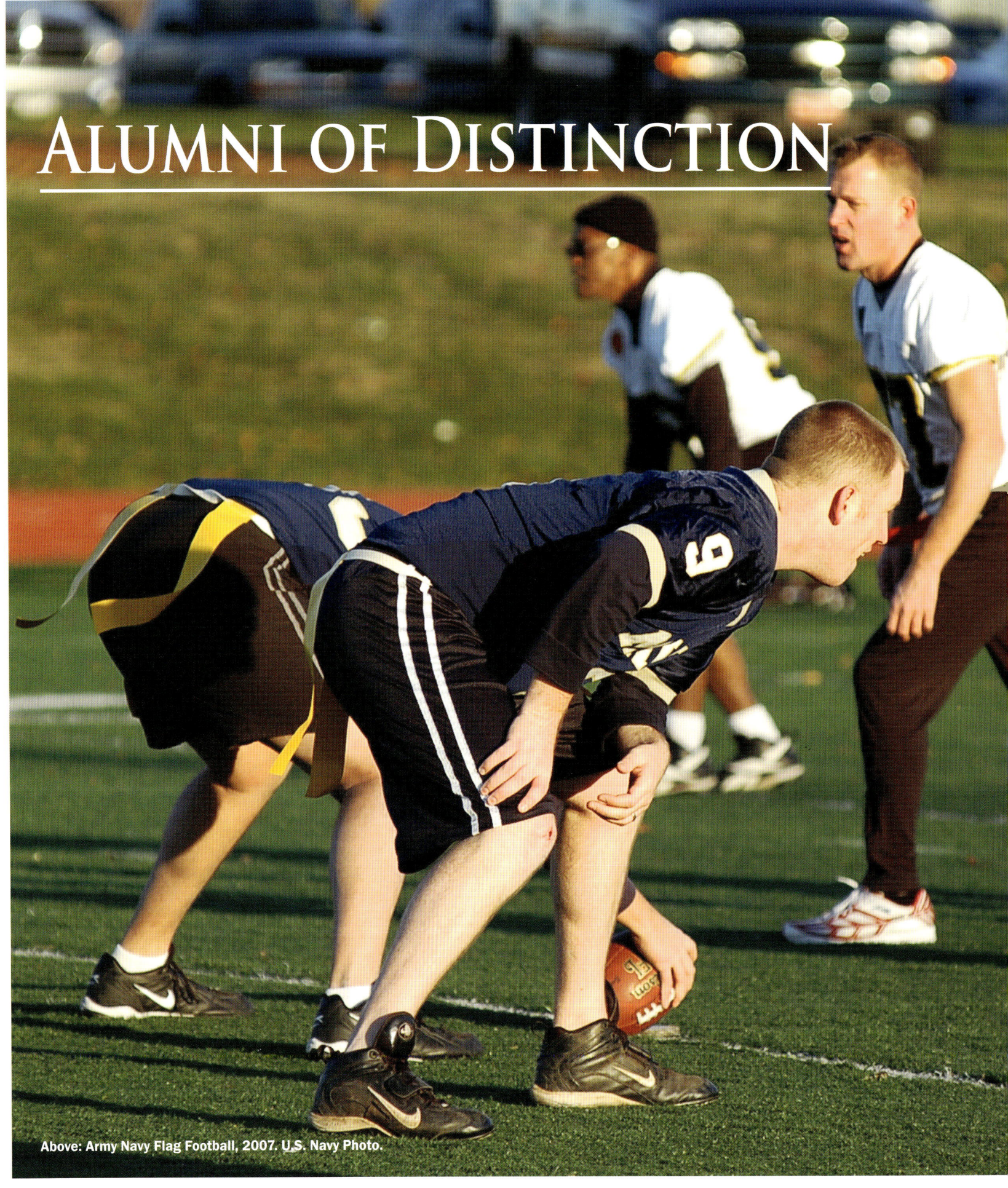

Above: Army Navy Flag Football, 2007. U.S. Navy Photo.

ALUMNI OF DISTINCTION

Photo # 80-G-466244 Adm. Chester W. Nimitz, USN, circa 1942

"The war with Japan had been reenacted in the game rooms at the Naval War College by so many people, and in so many different ways, that nothing that happened during the war was a surprise . . . absolutely nothing except the kamikaze tactics toward the end of the war; we had not visualized these."

Fleet Admiral Chester W. Nimitz, U.S. Navy
Commander in Chief Pacific Forces during World War II,
Naval War College Class of 1920

Above: Admiral Nimitz, circa 1945. U.S. Navy History Photo.

Distinguished Graduate Leadership Award

The Distinguished Graduate Leadership Award, established in 1996, is presented to a graduate of the Naval War College whose accomplishments as a military leader and outstanding service in the national interest have brought honor to the nation, the United States Armed Forces, and the Naval War College. The award is sponsored by the Naval War College Foundation.

1996
GEN John M. Shalikashvili, USA
Chairman of the Joint Chiefs of Staff
College of Naval Command and Staff, 1970

1997
ADM Joseph W. Prueher, USN
Commander-in-Chief, U.S. Pacific Command
College of Naval Command and Staff, 1973

1998
ADM Robert E. Kramek, USCG
Commandant, United States Coast Guard
College of Naval Warfare, 1981

1999
GEN Charles E. Wilhelm, USMC
Commander, United States Southern Command
College of Naval Warfare, 1983
(Highest Distinction)

2000
VADM Robert J. Natter, USN
Deputy Chief of Naval Operations Plans,
Policy and Operations (N3/N5)
College of Naval Warfare, 1987
(With Distinction)

2001
ADM William J. Fallon, USN
Vice Chief of Naval Operations
College of Naval Command and Staff, 1978
(Highest Distinction)

2002
COL Charles J. Precourt, USAF (Ret.)
Chief of Astronaut Corps
College of Naval Command and Staff, 1990
(Highest Distinction)

2003
ADM Gregory G. Johnson, USN
Commander, U.S. Naval Forces, Europe
Commander, Allied Forces, Southern Europe
College of Naval Command and Staff, 1975
(Highest Distinction)

2004
GEN Michael W. Hagee, USMC
Commandant, U.S. Marine Corps
College of Naval Warfare, 1987
(With Distinction)

2005
The Honorable Christopher R. Hill
Assistant Secretary, Bureau of East Asian Pacific Affairs
College of Naval Warfare, 1994
(With Distinction)

2006
VADM David L. Brewer III, USN
Military Sealift Command
College of Naval Warfare, 1994

2007
ADM James G. Stavridis, USN
Commander, United States Southern Command
College of Continuing Education, 1985
(With Distinction)

2008
GEN James E. Cartwright, USMC
Vice Chairman, Joint Chiefs of Staff
College of Naval Warfare, 1991

2009
GEN Raymond T. Odierno, USA
Commanding General, Multi-National Force–Iraq

ALUMNI OF DISTINCTION

2009 Distinguished Graduate Leadership Award recipient GEN Raymond Odierno, U.S. Army, receives a painted slate from RADM James P. "Phil" Wisecup, U.S. Navy, as Master of Ceremonies Professor John Jackson reads the inscription.

2005 Distinguished Graduate Leadership Award recipient Ambassador Christopher R. Hill speaks to Naval War College students and faculty at the awards dinner held at the Washington Navy Yard. Ambassador Hill is now the U.S. Ambassador to Iraq.

Chief of the Astronaut Corps, COL Charles Precourt, U.S. Air Force, discusses the glove from his space suit at the 2002 Distinguished Graduate Leadership Award dinner.

DGLA display for Ambassador Hill in Conolly Hall stairwell.

General James E. Cartwright, U.S. Marine Corps, Vice Chairman of the Joint Chiefs of Staff, receives the DGLA award in 2008. U.S. Marine Corps Photo.

Above: RADM Jacob Shuford and NWC Foundation Board of Trustees Chairman John D'Luhy present Admiral James Stavridis with his DGLA certificate in 2007. U.S. Navy Photo.

CHIEFS OF NAVAL OPERATIONS

The Chief of Naval Operations is the senior military officer of the Department of the Navy. The Chief of Naval Operations is a four-star admiral and is responsible to the Secretary of the Navy for the command, utilization of resources, and operating efficiency of the operating forces of the Navy and of the Navy shore activities. A member of the Joint Chiefs of Staff, the Chief of Naval Operations is the principal naval adviser to the President and to the Secretary of the Navy on the conduct of war, and is the principal adviser and naval executive to the Secretary on the conduct of activities of the Department of the Navy. Assistants are the Vice Chief of Naval Operations, the Deputy Chiefs of Naval Operations, the Assistant Chiefs of Naval Operations and a number of other ranking officers. These officers and their staffs are collectively known as the Office of the Chief of Naval Operations. The following list of Chiefs of Naval Operations is annotated to identify those who are NWC graduates.

	Chief of Naval Operations	**Tenure**	**Naval War College**
1	ADM William S. Benson	May 11, 1915–September 25, 1919	Class of 1906
2	ADM Robert E. Coontz	November 1, 1919–July 21, 1923	
3	ADM Edward W. Eberle	July 21, 1923–November 14, 1927	Class of 1913
4	ADM Charles F. Hughes	November 14, 1927–September 17, 1930	Class of 1924
5	ADM William V. Pratt	September 17, 1930–June 30, 1933	Staff, 1911–13 NWC President, 1925–27
6	ADM William H. Standley	July 1, 1933–January 1, 1937	Class of 1921
7	ADM William D. Leahy	January 2, 1937–August 1, 1939	
8	ADM Harold R. Stark	August 1, 1939–March 2, 1942	Class of 1923
9	FADM Ernest J. King	March 2, 1942–December 15, 1945	Class of 1933
10	FADM Chester W. Nimitz	December 15, 1945–December 15, 1947	Class of 1923
11	ADM Louis E. Denfeld	December 15, 1947–November 2, 1949	
12	ADM Forrest P. Sherman	November 2, 1949–July 22, 1951	Class of 1927
13	ADM William M. Fechteler	August 16, 1951–August 17, 1953	
14	ADM Robert B. Carney	August 17, 1953–August 17, 1955	
15	ADM Arleigh A. Burke	August 17, 1955 August 1, 1961	Correspondence
16	ADM George W. Anderson Jr.	August 1, 1961–August 1, 1963	
17	ADM David L. McDonald	August 1, 1963–August 1, 1967	
18	ADM Thomas H. Moorer	August 1, 1967–July 1, 1970	Class of 1953
19	ADM Elmo R. Zumwalt	July 1, 1970–June 29, 1974	Class of 1953
20	ADM James L. Holloway III	June 29, 1974–July 1, 1978	
21	ADM Thomas B. Hayward	July 1, 1978–June 30, 1982	Class of 1959
22	ADM James D. Watkins	June 30, 1982–June 30, 1986	
23	ADM Carlisle A.H. Trost	July 1, 1986–June 29, 1990	
24	ADM Frank B. Kelso II	June 29, 1990–April 23, 1994	
25	ADM Jeremy M. Boorda	April 23, 1994–May 16, 1996	Class of 1971
26	ADM Jay L. Johnson	May 16, 1996–July 21, 2000	
27	ADM Vern Clark	July 21, 2000–July 22, 2005	
28	ADM Michael Mullen	July 22, 2005–September 29, 2007	
29	ADM Gary Roughead	September 29, 2007–*Present*	

President Bush Addresses International Alumni

The Naval War College played host to the 43rd President of the United States, The Honorable George W. Bush, on 28 June 2007. The occasion was the International Maritime Symposium and the 50th Reunion of the senior program for international officers, the Naval Command College. Speaking to an overflow crowd of students, faculty, staff members and over 230 reunion participants from 41 different countries, President Bush spoke at length about the success of U.S. military and diplomatic activities in Iraq and Afghanistan. Arriving in Rhode Island aboard Air Force One, he was met by Rhode Island Governor Don Carcieri, who accompanied the President aboard Marine One for a helicopter tour of Newport Harbor, where more than two dozen sailing ships from 19 nations were gathered for an event known as TALL SHIPS 2007. While at NWC, the President spent more than two hours speaking in small private groups to the families of service members who had died in the War on Terror. In past years, NWC has been visited by many U.S. Presidents, including George H.W. Bush, John Kennedy, Dwight Eisenhower, and Theodore Roosevelt.

Photos by MCC Greg Frazho.

ALUMNI OF DISTINCTION

RADM Wisecup and Congressman Patrick Kennedy (D-RI) in conversation in Quarters "A." U.S. Navy Photo.

"My Naval War College experience was tremendously valuable for a number of reasons. It allowed me to open my professional aperture by introducing me to the operational and strategic levels of war, and gave me for the first time a comprehensive view of the true complexities of our business. It solidified the idea of 'the joint fight,' and highlighted the 'leadership' imperative and its pivotal role in sometimes leveling the technological playing field.

"Perhaps as much as anything else, my training in Newport reinforced the importance of personal relationships . . . during the 15 years since attending NWC, I've been amazed at the number of times relationships forged that year with my Army, Navy, Marine Corps and Air Force classmates came into play. There is no question in my mind that my Naval War College experience made me a significantly better and more effective Naval officer and leader."

Rear Admiral Richard E. Cellon, USN (Ret.)
Former Commander, FIRST Naval Construction Division

Bibliography

Interviews

Cherpak, Evelyn. Personal Interview. 12 Jan 08.

Davis, Elizabeth T. Personal Interview. 12 Jan 08.

Gatchel, Theodore. Personal Interview. 4 Mar 08.

Hattendorf, John B. Personal Interview. 11 Dec 07.

Jackson, John. Personal Interview. 14 Jan 08.

Roughead, Gary. Email Interview. 1 Feb 08.

Sellers, Karen D. Personal Interview. 12 Jan 08.

Shuford, Jacob L. Personal Interview. 28 Feb 08.

Turner, Stansfield. Email Interview. 1 Feb 08.

Books and Journals

Bureau of Navigation, Department of the Navy. 1917. *Record of Medals of Honor Issued to the Officers and Enlisted Men of the United States Navy, Marine Corps and Coast Guard (1862–1917).* Washington: Government Printing Office.

Clark, Charles E. 1917. *My Fifty Years in the Navy.* Boston: Little, Brown, and Company.

Ellis, F. R. April 1964. The U.S. Naval War College Story. *Newport History: Bulletin of the Newport Historical Society,* Vol 37, No. 2. Newport: Franklin Printing House.

Field, Edward. 1898. *Esek Hopkins: Comander-in-Chief of the Continental Navy during the American Revolution 1775 to 1778.* Providence: The Preston & Rounds Co.

Fiske, Bradley A. 1919. *From Midshipman to Rear-Admiral.* The Century Co.

Hackett, Frank W. 1900. *An Address Delivered Before the Naval War College.* U.S. Government Printing Office.

Hattendorf, John B., Simpson III, B. Mitchell, and Wadleigh, John R. 1984. *Sailors and Scholars: The Centennial History of the U.S. Naval War College.* U.S. Government Printing Office.

Hollis, Ira N. 1900. *The Frigate CONSTITUTION: The Central Figure of the Navy Under Sail.* Boston and New York: Houghton, Mifflin and Company.

Kittredge, Tracy Barrett. 1921. *Naval Lessons of the Great War.* New York: Doubleday, Page and Company.

Books and Journals (Continued)

Long, John D. 1903. *The New American Navy.* New York: The Outlook Company.

Lossing, Benson J. 1881. *The Story of the United States Navy for Boys.* New York: Harper & Brothers.

Maclay, Edgar Stanton. 1902. *A History of the United States Navy From 1775 to 1902.* Volumes I, II, and III. New York: D. Appleton and Company.

Mahan, A. T. 1915. *Naval Strategy: Compared and Contrasted with the Principles and Practice of Military Operations on Land.* Boston: Little, Brown, and Company.

Meany, William Barry. 1911. *Commodore John Barry: The Father of the American Navy.* New York: Harper & Brothers Publishers.

Meisler, Stanley. 1997. *United Nations: The First Fifty Years.* New York: Atlantic Monthly Press.

Miller, Francis T. 1911. *The Photographic History of the Civil War in Ten Volumes.* New York: The Review of Reviews Co.

National Educational Association. 1904. *Journal of Proceedings and Addresses of the Forty-Third Annual Meeting.* Minnesota: National Educational Association.

Papers of Admiral Oscar C. Badger, USN, Operational Archives Branch, Naval Historical Center, Washington, D.C.

Perrien, Joseph. 1906. *Deeds of Valor.* Michigan: The Perrien-Keydel Company.

Poore, Perley (Editor). 1883. *Message from the President of the United States to the Two Houses of Congress at the Commencement of the First Session of the Forty-Eighth Congress, with Reports of the Heads of Departments.* Government Printing Office.

Sims, William S. September 1919. *The United States Naval War College.* United States Naval Institute *Proceedings*, Vol 45, No. 9, Pg 1485. Annapolis: U.S. Naval Institute. Repr., n.p., [1919?].

Stringer, Harry R. 1921. *The Navy Book of Distinguished Service.* Washington: Fassett Publishing Company.

Taylor, Charles Carlisle. 1920. *The Life of Admiral Mahan.* London: John Murray.

United States Bureau of Naval Personnel. 1950. *Medal of Honor, 1861–1949: The Navy.* Washington: Government Printing Office.

Wadleigh, John R. Summer 1983. Laying the Keel of the Naval War College. *Bulletin of the Newport Historical Society*, Vol 56, Part I, No. 191. Newport: Franklin Printing House.

Magazines

Snaza, Gregg L. January/February 1990. Inport Ship Savers. *Surface Warfare Magazine*.

Brochures

The Naval War College Museum. Naval War College Foundation.

The President's House. Naval War College Foundation.

The Settler's Stone. Naval War College Foundation.

Websites

Admiral Frank F. Fletcher, USN, (1855–1928). Naval Historical Center. http://www.history.navy.mil/photos/pers-us/uspers-f/ff-fltr.htm. Accessed on December 14, 2007.

Admiral Frank Jack Fletcher, USN (Retired), (1885–1973). Naval Historical Center. http://www.history.navy.mil/photos/pers-us/uspers-f/fj-fltr.htm. Accessed on December 14, 2007.

Air Force Link. http://www.af.mil/bios/. Accessed on December 15, 2007 to January 28, 2008.

Antrim. Naval Historical Center. http://www.history.navy.mil/danfs/a9/antrim-i.htm. Accessed on December 17, 2007.

Arlington Cemetery. http://www.arlingtoncemetery.net/obadger2.htm. Accessed on January 17, 2008.

Badger. Naval Historical Center. http://www.history.navy.mil/danfs/b1/badger-iii.htm. Accessed on December 3, 2007.

Captain Albert H. Rooks, USN, (1891–1942). Naval Historical Center. http://www.history.navy.mil/photos/pers-us/uspers-r/a-rooks.htm. Accessed on December 1 and 16, 2007.

Captain Franklin Van Valkenburgh, USN, (1888–1941). Naval Historical Center. http://www.history.navy.mil/photos/pers-us/uspers-v/f-vanvlk.htm. Accessed on December 4, 2007.

Captain Mervyn Sharp Bennion, USN, (1887–1941). Naval Historical Center. http://www.history.navy.mil/photos/pers-us/uspers-b/m-benion.htm. Accessed on December 1, 2007.

Home of Heroes. http://www.homeofheroes.com/a_homepage/community/misc/mccandless_family.htm. Accessed on December 14, 2007.

Italian Historical Society. http://www.italianhistorical.org/verrazzano.htm. Accessed on January 3, 2008.

Lieutenant Commander Walter A. Edwards, USN (1886–1928). Naval Historical Center. http://www.history.navy.mil/photos/pers-us/uspers-e/wa-edwds.htm. Accessed on December 14, 2007.

National Historic Landmarks Program. http://www.nps.gov/history/nhl/. Accessed on December 20, 2007.

National Register of Historic Places. http://www.nationalregisterofhistoricplaces.com. Accessed on January 3, 2008.

Naval Historical Center. http://www.history.navy.mil/. Accessed on December 15, 2007 to January 28, 2008.

Websites (Continued)

Rear Admiral Edwin A. Anderson, USN, (1860–1933). Naval Historical Center. http://www.history.navy.mil/photos/pers-us/uspers-a/e-andrsn.htm. Accessed on December 13, 2007.

Rear Admiral Isaac C. Kidd, USN, (1884–1941). Naval Historical Center. http://www.history.navy.mil/photos/pers-us/uspers-k/ic-kidd.htm. Accessed on December 14, 2007.

Rear Admiral Norman Scott, USN, (1889–1942). Naval Historical Center. http://www.history.navy.mil/photos/pers-us/uspers-s/n-scott.htm. Accessed on December 6, 2007.

Rear Admiral Richard H. O'Kane, USN-Retired (1911–1994). Naval Historical Center. http://www.history.navy.mil/photos/pers-us/uspers-o/rh-okane.htm. Accessed on December 1, 2007.

Rear Admiral Samuel G. Fuqua, USN, (1899–1987). Naval Historical Center. http://www.history.navy.mil/photos/pers-us/uspers-f/s-fuqua.htm. Accessed on December 1, 2007.

Upshur. Naval Historical Center. http://www.history.navy.mil/danfs/u1/upshur-i.htm. Accessed on December 12, 2007.

US Naval Academy. http://www.usna.edu/PAO/Photos/StockdaleWhites.jpg. Accessed on December 14, 2007.

USS Bradley. http://www.ussbradley.com/WWBradley.htm. Accessed on December 14, 2007.

Vice Admiral Harry McL. P. Huse, USN, (1858–1942). Naval Historical Center. http://www.history.navy.mil/photos/pers-us/uspers-h/hmp-huse.htm. Accessed on December 1, 2007.

William R. Rush. Naval Historical Center. http://www.history.navy.mil/danfs/w9/william_r_rush.htm. Accessed on December 14, 2007.

William Rush. http://williamrrush.org/WmRushBio.htm. Accessed on February 1, 2008.

Naval War College Review

Shuford, Jacob L. President's Forum. Summer 2005. *The Naval War College's Twin Missions.*

———. President's Forum. Autumn 2005. *Shaping the Future.*

———. President's Forum. Summer 2006. *Creating a Thousand-Ship Navy.*

———. President's Forum. Autumn 2006. *A New Maritime Strategy: Admiral Mullen's Challenge.*

———. President's Forum. Winter 2007. *Toward a Coherent Education Strategy in the Navy.*

———. President's Forum. Spring 2007. *An International Forum for Operational and Strategic Leadership.*

———. President's Forum. Autumn 2007. *Our Citizen-Sailors and Professional Military Education.*

———. President's Forum. Winter 2008. *A Cooperative Strategy for 21st Century Seapower.*